The Feeling Economy

"AI is already turning our world upside down, taking over much of thinking and decision making that used to be the privilege of humans. And you ain't seen nothing yet. Don't be scared! Business professors Rust and Huang are the perfect guides who lead you through the uncharted territory of this enormous transformation. Their conclusion? The outcome will be a 'Feeling Economy' that provides new opportunities for everybody who acts on one simple fact: in the future AI will do the thinking, and humans will do the feeling. This extraordinary book provides you with the insights and skills to stay ahead in the Feeling Economy rather than be left behind."

—Bernd Schmitt, *Robert D. Calkins Professor of International Business,*
Columbia University

"This book is an easy to read and fast-paced book that provides a framework for thinking about how AI will change not only the economy, but everyday life. They describe how the advance of AI capabilities is changing jobs, education, politics, governance and ethics. Rust and Huang are leading business scholars, so they also provide a roadmap for the managerial implications of AI. They have packaged timely and accessible information, and then seasoned it all with just the right amount of provocative opinions, intended to get the reader thinking in a new way about their hopes, dreams and fears about our future with AI."

—Jim Spohrer, *Director of Cognitive OpenTech, IBM*

"This book by award-winning business scholars, Rust and Huang, focuses on the human implications of the development of AI. Using a simple but powerful conceptualization of the levels of intelligence of AI (from mechanical, to thinking, to feeling), the book shows how AI is increasingly assuming thinking tasks, pushing humans (both managers and consumers) toward a focus on interpersonal relationships and empathy. The shift in economic processes from physical goods to services, and intersection of the service economy with the levels of intelligence is uniquely captured. The book highlight the fundamental cognitive implications of AI growth with respect to prior technological waves. The book is accessible and profound. This book gives a practical roadmap to provide a nuanced understanding on the opportunities and potential threats of AI growth for societal consideration."

—Saurabh Mishra, *Director of the AI Index Program, Stanford Institute for*
Human-Centered Artificial Intelligence (HAI)

Roland T. Rust · Ming-Hui Huang

The Feeling Economy

How Artificial Intelligence Is Creating the Era of Empathy

Roland T. Rust
University of Maryland
College Park, MD, USA

Ming-Hui Huang
National Taiwan University
Taipei, Taiwan

ISBN 978-3-030-52976-5   ISBN 978-3-030-52977-2   (eBook)
https://doi.org/10.1007/978-3-030-52977-2

© The Editor(s) (if applicable) and The Author(s), under exclusive licence to Springer Nature Switzerland AG, part of Springer Nature 2021
This work is subject to copyright. All rights are solely and exclusively licensed by the Publisher, whether the whole or part of the material is concerned, specifically the rights of translation, reprinting, reuse of illustrations, recitation, broadcasting, reproduction on microfilms or in any other physical way, and transmission or information storage and retrieval, electronic adaptation, computer software, or by similar or dissimilar methodology now known or hereafter developed.
The use of general descriptive names, registered names, trademarks, service marks, etc. in this publication does not imply, even in the absence of a specific statement, that such names are exempt from the relevant protective laws and regulations and therefore free for general use.
The publisher, the authors and the editors are safe to assume that the advice and information in this book are believed to be true and accurate at the date of publication. Neither the publisher nor the authors or the editors give a warranty, expressed or implied, with respect to the material contained herein or for any errors or omissions that may have been made. The publisher remains neutral with regard to jurisdictional claims in published maps and institutional affiliations.

This Palgrave Macmillan imprint is published by the registered company Springer Nature Switzerland AG
The registered company address is: Gewerbestrasse 11, 6330 Cham, Switzerland

To all my loving Maltese doggies, Joy, Sweetie, Leo, Lisa, Buddy (aka "Baddy" or "Little"), Minnie, and many in the memories, for your love and great feeling intelligence.

Ming-Hui

To my 91-year-old mother, who I promised would be able to read most of this book, to my brilliant wife, and to all the other strong and empathetic women who will lead us in the next era of AI. (Also to the dogs, so I don't get in trouble with my wife.)

Roland

Preface

Artificial intelligence (AI) is profoundly changing our world, in ways that are not yet well-understood, because of the implicit (and wrong) assumption that all AI is about thinking intelligence. If we realize that there are multiple intelligences, of differing difficulty for AI, and that this is what drives the order of AI development, then we start to understand how this will change the balance between AI and HI (human intelligence). What AI has done so far is only a taste of what is to come. As AI advances further, this will change everything. It is already changing the world in predictable and measurable ways. The advance of thinking AI will usher in a Feeling Economy in which AI does much of the thinking, and humans need to scramble to do whatever they are still better at, which is tasks that involve feeling intelligence and interpersonal relationships. This will turn just about everything upside down, including the educational system. Our book is intended to help us understand these changes.

At the time of this writing, we are in the midst of a coronavirus pandemic. Public health scientists warn that such pandemics are likely to become more numerous, due to human encroachment of the natural world, increased global travel, and crowded cities that facilitate the spread of such viruses. The response to all of this is likely to lead to an increased use of AI by everyone, for health and for personal reasons. This implies that the development of AI, together with pandemics, are likely to accelerate the coming of the Feeling Economy. We have an even stronger need for empathy to help support each other in difficult times, and we need to be even more empathetic with each other. The current health crisis only strengthens our prediction: AI is creating the era of empathy; thus, the Feeling Economy is coming.

College Park, USA   Roland T. Rust
Taipei, Taiwan   Ming-Hui Huang
June 2020

Acknowledgements

We are grateful to many colleagues and collaborators who have helped us to develop our thinking on the development of artificial intelligence and its implications. We cannot mention everyone, but especially would like to thank several co-authors whose work has been featured in this book. Finance professor Max Maksimovic, our co-author on *The Feeling Economy* article in the *California Management Review* AI special issue, believed our idea that the Feeling Economy is coming since the beginning, and helped us empirically validate it. Michael Haenlein, a colleague who is also an AI researcher, supported the idea of the Feeling Economy, while many other editors and scholars still implicitly believe the Thinking Economy will be here forever. Tuck-Siong Chung and Michel Wedel, in their joint work with Rust on adaptive personalization systems, inspired the idea of how thinking AI would facilitate personalization, which sets the basis for relationalization, the major benefit people are looking for in the Feeling Economy. Kalinda Ukanwa, Roland's former doctoral student, now an assistant professor at University of Southern California, helped inspire the thinking about the costs of AI-based discrimination. We thank Tom Brown and Mike Brady, whose Organizational Frontlines Research Symposium (OFR) inspired Huang about the importance of Feeling AI, and Jim Spohrer, whose broad perspective, technical knowledge, and real-world orientation have been inspirational for a broad view about the societal and economic impact of AI. Thanks also to Tor Andreassen and Charles Colby, whose efforts have helped to advance our work. We cannot mention everyone, but we are also grateful to our other co-authors whose work has been featured in this book. Thanks also to Jamison Sheffer, Tassilo von Bohlen und Halbach, and Pranav Deo, who helped with background research. Thanks to the attendees at the Frontiers in Service Conference in Singapore, the Winter American Marketing Association Conference in San Diego, the Conference on AI, Machine Learning & Business Analytics in Philadelphia, the Artificial Intelligence and Robots in Service Interactions conference in Zaragoza, Spain, and the Theory and Practice in Marketing Conference in New York City for their helpful comments. We also thank our students at the University of Maryland and National Taiwan University whose insights and discussion have stimulated our thinking. Special thanks, also, to Marcus Ballenger from Palgrave, who encouraged us to write the book, and to Sophia Siegler for her help in the production process. Thanks to the Ministry of Science and Technology, Taiwan for financial support (grants 106-2410-H-002-056-MY3 and 107-2410-H-002-115-MY3). We are certain that we have inadvertently left out many others who deserved to be recognized. We apologize for that, and thank them equally.

Contents

List of Figures

List of Tables

1

Introduction

Artificial Intelligence (AI) is not just science fiction anymore. It already permeates our daily lives, changing how we seek and use information, and taking over many of our tasks. Whenever we use the Google search engine, or ask Alexa a question, we are interacting with AI. How we live our lives, and how we work, are being profoundly transformed by AI. Ironically, as AI is becoming more able to think, human intelligence (HI) is deemphasizing thinking in favor of feeling and interpersonal relationships. The result is a "Feeling Economy," in which AI and HI will collaborate closely—AI will do more of the thinking, and HI will emphasize feeling.

Stages of Development of AI

To understand why this is happening, we need to consider the order of development of AI. Roughly speaking, there are three levels of intelligence for AI—mechanical, thinking, and feeling. Mechanical AI refers to the mechanical or repetitive tasks that can be mechanized and standardized. The car-making robots that dominate modern automobile factories are examples of mechanical AI. Mechanical is the "easiest" level of AI intelligence, and many analysts still wrongly assume that the potential of AI is limited to repetitive tasks.

Before AI made serious inroads, we were in a "Physical Economy" in which most humans were involved with physical labor. This economy dominated through most of the nineteenth century. The industrial revolution brought primitive AI into the workplace, and began the uneasy relationship between

© The Author(s) 2021
R. T. Rust and M.-H. Huang, *The Feeling Economy*,
https://doi.org/10.1007/978-3-030-52977-2_1

AI and HI. As AI assumed more mechanical tasks, however, the humans who used to perform those tasks were displaced. Factory workers, farmworkers, miners, and other manual, blue-collar workers found their skills to be obsolete. Mechanical AI brought in a "Thinking Economy" in which both consumers and workers put more emphasis on thinking tasks, and performed less physical labor.

In the Thinking Economy, which mostly characterizes our current moment circa 2020, the predominant work tasks are thinking tasks, and it is assumed that the purpose of education is to teach people how to think effectively. At the same time, thinking AI is a topic of rapid research development. AI products like IBM's Watson seek to augment workers by taking over more of their thinking tasks. This will also displace thinking workers, who will need to demonstrate "higher" intelligence (meaning a level of intelligence harder for AI to emulate). In other words, thinking AI is replacing many human thinking tasks, leaving HI to focus on feeling and interpersonal relationships. When those feeling tasks become more important across the economy than thinking tasks, we will have entered the "Feeling Economy." We will see later that our best estimate for when the Feeling Economy will become more important than the Thinking Economy is the year 2036, although the shift toward the Feeling Economy is already well underway.

The Nature of the Feeling Economy

The Feeling Economy emphasizes emotion and empathy. It is hardly a coincidence that the proliferation of emoticons (emoji) has occurred during the time of the emerging Feeling Economy. People everywhere are seeking to express emotion more quickly and efficiently. Consumers who can no longer multiply two numbers together can nevertheless draw upon an extensive menu of possible emotional symbols to communicate. The former thinking machines are now emotional beings.

In the Feeling Economy, the nature of jobs will change. Let us consider the job of Financial Analyst, for example. What seems like a very thinking-intensive analytical job is, in fact, becoming more feeling-oriented. As one financial analyst told us, he leaves the technical stuff to AI now, and focuses instead on client relationships, hand-holding, and reassurance. This shift toward feeling is happening across the economy. Consider, for example, the job of customer service representative. In the old days, the customer service rep would actually answer the telephone. Today, on the other hand, the routine questions are typically handled by an AI chatbot. The customer service rep only deals with nonroutine issues. Fewer customer service reps are needed, but those remaining have been "upgraded" to focus on tasks that involve judgment, creativity, intuition, emotion, empathy, and people skills—the things AI currently has more trouble doing.

One likely outcome of the Feeling Economy is that women will become more important in the economy. This is due to women, on average, having better empathy and people skills. This is not to say that men can't also have good people skills (just as there are women who are good factory workers). On average, though, we can expect women to have an advantage. This can result in societal displacement. For example, when thinking AI ended the Physical Economy, many men (who had a physical advantage, on average, in size and strength) were displaced, leaving many unemployed men in factory towns, coal country, and farm country. Thus, Donald Trump's pick for the Fed stated that the biggest problem in the economy was the decline in male earnings. Just as men were displaced when the Physical Economy gave way to the Thinking Economy, women may have the edge over men in the Feeling Economy.

As thinking AI assumes more of the thinking tasks, humans will become less adept at thinking, and focus more on feeling. We are already seeing evidence of these shifts in many arenas, including politics. Donald Trump, for example, was the least thinking-oriented Presidential candidate in many years. Hillary Clinton came across as much more intelligent and better-informed. From a thinking intelligence standpoint, Hillary was the winner, hands down. She lost, however, primarily because she did not connect to people emotionally the way Trump (or even her husband, former President Bill Clinton) did. Trump had no clear solutions, but he highlighted people's disillusionment and alienation. Similar "populist" candidates are springing up around the world, seen in phenomena such as Brexit in the United Kingdom, the Five Star Movement in Italy, and the election of a comedian as President of Ukraine.

As the work world changes, education must also change, to keep up. It is implicitly assumed at every level of education that education is about training people to think. In the Feeling Economy, this may not be the right thing. If career success is going to hinge mostly on emotion, empathy, and people skills, then education needs to gravitate toward those subjects. Instead of Data Science 101 maybe the courses of the future will be "Introduction to Empathy," "Emotional Intelligence," and "Collaborating with AI." Sure, there will need to be a few world-class intellectuals who can be the technologists who interact with the AI algorithms, but most people will find better success by gravitating toward the "softer" side. Admission of students to graduate business programs, for example, might increasingly emphasize group experience and people skills, and deemphasize markers of analytical intelligence such as the math GRE or GMAT.

Management will be best off thinking of AI and HI as a team, and making sure that each focuses on its area of highest competence. That is, AI will be the thinking partner, and HI will be the feeling partner. As the thinking tasks are removed from human jobs, those jobs will need to be redesigned to be more feeling-oriented and people-focused. This will also change the candidate set for filling these jobs—the "geek" or "nerd" currently filling a Thinking Economy job may need to focus on developing more people skills, as sheer analytical firepower is becoming deemphasized.

How the Feeling Economy Affects Consumers and Society

It is not just the workers and jobs that are changing. The everyday consumer is changing, too. With smartphones and other devices now doing much of the thinking work, even consumers are becoming more feeling-oriented. We see this from the proliferation of social media. Even if not all "friends" are really friends, there is still an unprecedented degree of connection between people, with the associated potential for emotion, empathy, and interpersonal relationships. The implication for management is that we cannot assume any longer that the consumer is rational. In psychology they talk about the "central route" and "peripheral route" to persuasion, with the implicit assumption that the more rational "central route" is the more important of the two. In the Feeling Economy, this is turned on its head. The less rational "peripheral route" is now the more important, and marketers ignore emotion at their own peril.

The Feeling Economy, like the Thinking Economy before it, will have winners and losers. The thinking workers displaced by thinking AI will be an important problem for society, just like the physical workers displaced by mechanical AI. Thinking AI is driven by capital, and it is meaningful to consider the inequality effects that are similar to those when mechanical AI took over. AI operates at scale, which means capitalists who implement AI can get very, very rich, while those displaced by AI can fall behind economically. This has caused some in the Silicon Valley tech community to advocate a universal basic income. That is, everybody gets a minimum income, whether they are working or not. Such a plan has clear advantages (e.g., preventing extreme poverty) as well as disadvantages (e.g., removing incentive to work).

Looking Forward

We are currently experiencing the emergence of the Feeling Economy. What happens, though, when AI develops even better skills, enabling AI to be creative, or even to develop feeling skills? Actually, there is considerable ongoing research to build creative AI. In fact, creative AI is already ubiquitous, but mostly in the context of collaborating with humans. For example, modern popular music typically contains electronics (e.g., synthesizers, sequencers and drum machines) that are programmed by computer. The human aspect in such music is often limited to the singing—sometimes there is no direct human playing of instruments at all. In other words, the most emotional aspect of music, the human voice, is about all that remains in the human sphere in a lot of today's popular music.

It is probably a mistake, then, to assume that creativity is a lasting safe haven for human workers. In fact, there are already examples of musical pieces and prose and poetry that are exclusively written by computers. There will be more to come.

It also seems foolish to write off AI's capabilities when it comes to feeling. The great AI pioneer, Alan Turing, developed his famous Turing test as a way of testing AI. In the Turing test, if a human observer can't tell the difference between AI behavior vs. human behavior, then AI is as good as human. For feeling AI to pass the Turing test, it needs to (1) recognize human emotion accurately and (2) respond in an emotionally appropriate way. There is already active research in both of these areas, and successful implementation in practice is only a matter of time. Google, as well as many academic researchers, are developing methods to read people's emotions from their facial expressions. Similarly, research on chatbots is developing ability to recognize emotion in speech. Responding emotionally is also under active development. Already, there are many robots, such as the University of Auckland's Baby X, that are quite convincing in expressing emotions. One such robot, Sophia, has already been named a citizen of the nation of Saudi Arabia.

Looking deeper into the future, once feeling AI is well-established, AI will likely be better than HI at everything. This is the "singularity," as proposed by Ray Kurzweil. Prospects for humans at that point involve either turning AI into our servants (AI does all the work, and humans have only leisure time), merging with AI (e.g., humans become cyborgs), or becoming irrelevant (e.g., AI wins, humans scrounge for scraps). Although it is reassuring to imagine us continuing to be in charge of AI, such an outcome seems unlikely if AI dominates us in all phases of intelligence. We conclude that beyond the Feeling Economy may involve even more displacement than the Feeling Economy, but at least that time appears to be several decades away.

Outline of the Book

Chapters 2–4 describe the three eras that result from AI, "The Physical Economy," (Chapter 2) "The Thinking Economy" (Chapter 3) and "The Feeling Economy," (Chapter 4) showing how these eras result from the level of development of AI. Chapters 5–11 describe the nature of the Feeling Economy. "The Age of Emoji," (Chapter 5) describes the emerging, emotionally charged era, "Jobs that Feel" (Chapter 6) discusses how human jobs are changing, "The Era of Women" (Chapter 7) predicts an era of heightened status for women in the Feeling Economy, "Politics that Feel" (Chapter 8) explores that changing ways that people choose politicians in the Feeling Economy, "How Education Must Change" (Chapter 9) describes how the Feeling Economy will transform education, "AI for Consumers" (Chapter 10) shows how the lives of everyday people are being transformed by AI, and "Management in the Feeling Economy" (Chapter 11) shows how management will need to change in the new environment. Chapter 12, "Moral, Ethical and Governance Implications," discusses how society might cope with the dislocations caused by the Feeling Economy.

Chapters 13–16 look forward from the Feeling Economy. "Artificial Creativity" (Chapter 13) discusses research efforts and early attempts to use AI to enhance creativity. "AI for Feeling" (Chapter 14) summarizes the research that tries to build AI that can reliably recognize emotion and respond in an emotionally appropriate manner. "Beyond the Feeling Economy" (Chapter 15) discusses the concept of the singularity—the point at which AI is better than HI at everything (physical, thinking, and feeling)—and considers both hopeful outcomes as well as apocalyptic ones. Chapter 16, "Conclusions," wraps up the book.

2

The Physical Economy

Looking back 100+ years, we see a very different economy than we have in today's developed nations. The economy then was based on sectors like manufacturing, farming, and mining. This was the Physical Economy. As the Thinking Economy unfolded, many who had prospered in the Physical Economy have been left behind. This has led to a nostalgia for the good old days in regions that boomed in the Physical Economy. But is it really possible to return to those days? For example, is it really possible to bring manufacturing jobs back to the United States?

Such a prospect is politically appealing. Voters from states that have traditionally depended on manufacturing, such as Michigan, Ohio, Pennsylvania, and Wisconsin, are desperate to regain their former prosperity, and are susceptible to politicians who will promise them that. For example, US President Donald Trump promised that he was going to bring manufacturing back to the United States. Starting in 2018, he imposed tariffs on Chinese imports, mostly manufacturing goods, to try to boost domestic manufacturing. China then retaliated with tariffs on US goods such as chemicals, vegetables, whiskey, and soybeans. The tariffs have hurt American workers, and the efforts to attract manufacturing have mostly failed. Even if those efforts were successful, the effect on manufacturing jobs would be diminished, because of the ability of AI to automate manufacturing. This causes us to question whether the economy of the nineteenth century can really be brought back to life in the information- and service-based twenty-first century.

In this chapter, we discuss the Physical Economy, an economy that existed before the revolution in information and communications technologies.

© The Author(s) 2021
R. T. Rust and M.-H. Huang, *The Feeling Economy,*
https://doi.org/10.1007/978-3-030-52977-2_2

Roughly speaking, this is the economy of the nineteenth century and before. Can we bring it back, or is it desirable to bring it back, when technologies have advanced from manufacturing technologies (e.g., assembly lines), to information technologies (e.g., such as ATM to automate front-end service interactions and enterprise resource planning [ERP] to automate back-office functions), to artificial intelligence (AI) (e.g., smart and autonomous systems to automate front-end interactions such as chatbots and greeting robots, and back-end data analytics)?

To be able to answer this question, we need to know what an economy is and how it evolves. An economy is how goods and services are produced and consumed. Producing these goods and services requires input of resources such as labor (unskilled or skilled) and capital (e.g., machinery, information technology, or AI). Whether to use more labor or machinery (i.e., technology) and which types of labor or machinery to use as production inputs determine what kind of economy we have.

An economy evolves due to advances in technology, which have tended to move from manufacturing technologies, to information technologies, to AI. The Physical Economy is one that dominated in the mid-nineteenth century, spanning the first and second industrial revolutions, powered by machinery, in which manufacturing first became prominent. Even today, many people refer to the most advanced economies as "industrial," even though the most advanced parts of the economy have moved beyond that. In the Physical Economy, employment and wages are more attributable to mechanical tasks, such as inspecting equipment or material, performing general physical activities, and repairing and maintaining equipment. The technological driving force for the Physical Economy is manufacturing technology (or machinery); machines that provide tools to enable production of all manufactured goods.

Most of the developed economies have moved away from the Physical Economy and are in the Thinking Economy today, due to the revolution in information technology (IT), in which the service sector dominates. Now with the continuing advancement of technology from IT to AI, the economy is advancing even further, toward the Feeling Economy, in which "hard service" sectors (those service sectors that mainly require hard thinking skills, such as scientific thinking and analytical skills) are beginning to give way to "soft service" sectors (those service sectors that emphasize soft, social, people skills and human touch, such as healthcare, hospitality, and education).

One may wonder, is the Physical (manufacturing) Economy really in the past, because we still see manufacturing here and there, such as automobile manufacturing in Michigan, food and beverage manufacturing in North Carolina, and motor vehicle parts manufacturing in Indiana. Even more manufacturing is done outside the United States, mostly in developing countries such as China.

Can, or should, we bring manufacturing back to the United States? In this chapter, we lay out a roadmap about how the economy evolves from physical, to thinking, to feeling, from the nineteenth century to the future, due to the advances of technology from machinery, to information technology, to artificial intelligence. This roadmap is developed from our series of papers based on both theoretical predictions and empirical evidence. It will help us to answer the question about whether we can, or should, go back to the manufacturing economy.

Multiple AI Intelligences

Machinery (manufacturing technology) is the pillar of the Physical Economy, information technology (mechanical AI) is the driving force of the Thinking Economy, and AI (cognitive technology) is the backbone of the Feeling Economy.

We translate these different technologies into a single view as "multiple AI intelligences." This view not only integrates different generational technologies under the AI umbrella, but also challenges the traditional thinking that there is only one intelligence, that is, thinking intelligence or intelligence quotient (IQ). The figure below shows this multiple AI intelligences view.

We often consider someone smart when he is good at math, science, or engineering, but less so when she is good at communicating and interacting with others. Being good at thinking intelligence, or IQ, is what most people think of as smart or genius. We hardly consider a person who can understand other people's pain (i.e., be empathetic) as smart; at most we would consider this person to be a nice person (many people's mothers and grandmothers would be considered "nice" rather than smart). This view is erroneous, because people can be emotionally intelligent, i.e., having high emotional quotient (EQ). It is a different type of intelligence, and comes naturally to some people (especially females who are mothers and caregivers), just as IQ comes naturally to some people.

Our multiple AI intelligences view emphasizes that, similar to the fact that humans have multiple intelligences, AI, designed to mimic human intelligences, should have multiple intelligences, too. Some people are good at thinking but poor at feeling (e.g., think of an eccentric, "geek" programmer, programming on his own), some are good at feeling but poor at thinking (e.g., think of some psychiatrists or friends who are great listeners), and

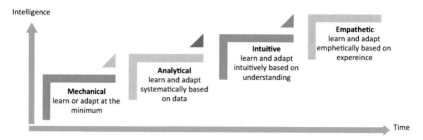

Fig. 2.1 Multiple AI Intelligences (*Source* Huang and Rust [2018], "Artificial Intelligence in Service," *Journal of Service Research*)

some are good at producing physical outputs (e.g., handymen, painters, and artists who produce wonderful pieces for us to enjoy). Those intelligences are distinct as well as overlapping. It is not necessary that one can only be good at one intelligence, but it may be more typical not to be good at all of them.

We first proposed this multiple AI intelligences view in our 2018 "Artificial Intelligence in Service" paper, in which AI intelligences are proposed to develop from mechanical, to analytical, to intuitive, and to empathetic, as illustrated in Fig. 2.1. This order is based on how difficult it is for AI to mimic that type of human intelligence. Mechanical intelligence is the easiest (for AI) level, and empathetic intelligence is the most difficult level. We later simplified the framework into three levels: from mechanical, to thinking, to feeling intelligence, in our 2019 "The Feeling Economy: Managing in the Next Era of AI" paper (*California Management Review*),[1] collapsing the analytical and intuitive levels into "thinking intelligence." We discuss the three levels of AI intelligences below.

Mechanical AI

Mechanical AI learns or adapts at most minimally. It does not learn all the time, either because it is unnecessary to learn (e.g., nothing new to learn, such as when tasks are repetitive and routine), or because it is undesirable to learn (e.g., for consistent and standard output over time). The distinction between mechanical AI and the traditional IT may not always be clear cut. We may consider IT as mechanical AI, because most IT is preprogramed to perform certain functions and is only updated when necessary. Learning or adaptive capability does not occur often or in real time. Most computer software can be viewed as mechanical AI. Some of us may feel that software updates are not really necessary, and we can manually disable the updates, indicating that learning and adaption are not necessary all the time.

Thinking AI

Thinking AI learns or adapts systematically, using cognitive data. Cognitive data are objective, and fact-based. Such data do not involve sentiment, feeling, emotions, preferences, attitudes, and contexts. They are typically "big," meaning that they are high in variety, velocity, and veracity—not just volume. Machine learning, neural networks, and deep learning (neural networks with additional layers) are some of the current major methods by which thinking AI learns and adapts. In Fig. 2.1, we further break down thinking AI into two subtypes: the lower-level analytical AI and the higher-level intuitive AI. We will discuss the two subtypes in Chapter 3, the Thinking Economy.

This is the level of AI intelligence that currently dominates the economy. Thinking AI booms due to the availability of big data, the advance of machine learning methods, the increase in computing power, and the decrease of computing costs; all these make data-based machine thinking feasible, efficient, and effective. In our 2014 *Marketing Science* paper, "The Service Revolution and the Transformation of Marketing Science," we documented how ubiquitous customer communication and big customer data transform and expand the economy into a service economy.[2] Essentially, the observation is that when technologies make data widely available as input of various machine learning algorithms and models, we are able to significantly expand our analytical, thinking capabilities, enabling closer relationships with customers.

Thinking AI can be considered a rational machine, because it generates output or makes decisions based on the systematic analysis of cognitive data. As defined above, ideally, cognitive data should be "neutral," meaning that the data do not contain any (emotional) bias. We will show later that this may not always be the case.

Feeling AI

This level of AI intelligence may be considered as qualitatively distinct from the thinking AI. It is like the contrast between EQ and IQ. Feeling (or empathetic, in the *JSR* paper) AI is not analytical or reasoning-based; instead, it learns and adapts from experience. The word "experience" implies that it is holistic, cannot be easily broken down into bytes of data, and cannot be easily separated from context; thus, this represents the highest level of AI intelligence that is most difficult for machines to mimic. Computer scientists are still struggling with how to develop feeling AI: should it be a straightforward extension of thinking AI, such as machine learning, but simply have emotional data as the input, or should it be an approach that is totally different from thinking AI? We don't have a conclusion yet, and major technology companies are competing on developing feeling AI, and treat it as a top trade secret.

For most humans, feeling intelligence may seem easy and effortless. We can see that a new-born baby cries immediately, and smiles when it is fed or when it sees its mother. For many people, this feeling type of intelligence does not require learning (and thus is under-appreciated). We rarely see that people go to universities to learn how to be empathetic. By contrast, it is thinking intelligence that most people and educational organizations emphasize. AI, on the other hand, has only rudimentary capabilities when it comes to feeling intelligence.

Empirical Evidence of Multiple AI Intelligences

This multiple AI intelligences view is supported by both theory and empirical evidence. Here we describe one piece of previously unpublished evidence. (Published evidence can be found in our 2019 *California Management Review* paper, "The Feeling Economy: Managing in the Next Generation of AI.") Using government data (The U.S. Bureau of Labor Statistics) from 2003 to 2016, we analyze the impact of four intelligences (i.e., the mechanical, analytical, intuitive, and empathetic intelligences required to get a task done) on a human worker's wages, while controlling for education (a proxy for the skill level required for a job). Table 2.1 shows the correlations between the five variables, based on about 11,000 observations. The larger the number,

Table 2.1 Means, standard deviations, and correlations among task intelligences and education

Intelligence level	1	2	3	4	5
1. Mechanical	1.00				
2. Analytical	0.15	1.00			
3. Intuitive	−0.08	0.81	1.00		
4. Feeling	−0.01	0.57	0.78	1.00	
5. Education	−0.37	0.54	0.71	0.42	1.00

Note Importance of intelligences to tasks are measured by importance ratings, ranging from 1 (not important) to 5 (very important) Education ranges from 1 (less than high school diploma) to 7 (doctoral or professional degree)
Source Authors' creation

the more similar (or dissimilar for the numbers with a "-" sign) the two variables are to each other. It is clear that education is negatively correlated with mechanical tasks, meaning that education is less important for mechanical intelligence. By contrast, education is positively correlated with the other three intelligences, especially with the two types of thinking intelligence—analytical and intuitive. This shows that our current educational system emphasizes training people to do thinking tasks.

We further compare the relative importance of the four intelligences to wages, while controlling for education (a proxy for thinking skills required for a job). The results are shown in Table 2.2. The star sign indicates how important the intelligence type is to wages. The more stars, the more significant the intelligence type's relationship to wages. Not surprisingly, we find that mechanical intelligence is no longer important to wages (not statistically significant, and even directionally negative). Analytical intelligence is the most important to wages, followed by intuitive intelligence and feeling intelligence.

When comparing the important differences between the task intelligences, we find some interesting results. The intelligences most important for wages are (over the time period of the study) analytical intelligence, intuitive intelligence, and feeling intelligence, in that order. Mechanical intelligence does not have a strong relationship with wages. This shows that mechanical intelligence, so important in the Physical Economy, is no longer as important. By extension, the Physical Economy itself is a backwater and a dead end, compared with the more dynamic parts of the economy. Note also that feeling intelligence is already almost as important as analytical intelligence and intuitive intelligence for wages.

The empirical evidence supports key elements of our theory: (1) there are multiple intelligences (applied to both humans and machines), as opposed

Table 2.2 The impact of task intelligences on wages

Predictors	Wage	
	Coefficient (z score)	Significance level
Mechanical tasks	−0.059 (−1.10)	
Analytical tasks	0.774 (9.90)	***
Intuitive tasks	0.631 (6.04)	***
Feeling tasks	0.516 (12.96)	***

Note ***$p < 0.000$
Source Authors' creation

to the dominant single thinking intelligence view and (2) mechanical intelligence no longer correlates with higher wages, while analytical, intuitive, and feeling intelligences all are important.

The empirical evidence also reveals that, except for mechanical intelligence, the importance of the other three intelligences to wages increases over time, especially the intuitive and feeling intelligences. This evidence can help us to form our conclusion about whether we can, or should, bring manufacturing back to the United States and other developed countries.

Manufacturing Technology (Machinery) for the Physical Economy

The Physical Economy is characterized by machinery that increases the productivity of human labor. This is the pre-AI economy. Manufacturing technology (machinery) provides the tools that enable production of all manufactured goods. Those tools magnify the effort of individual workers and give the economy power to turn raw materials into affordable, quality goods.[3]

History shows that different technologies play a key role in moving the economy forward. In the nineteenth century industrial revolution, assembly lines, and electricity-enabled large-scale mechanization, in which humans and machines work together to mass produce commodities efficiently (augmenting unskilled manufacturing labor). This is the economy for which economists formulated labor and capital as the two important input factors for the productivity of an economy.

As machinery began being used more widely in conjunction with human labor in production, the importance of human physical strength for production was reduced, but not eliminated. The most well-known manufacturing technology was assembly lines, a disruptive innovation by Henry Ford to mass produce cars efficiently. The great insight behind this innovation was that the complex automobile manufacturing process could be broken down into small pieces of simple, repetitive tasks; thus, any human worker without sophisticated skill training (without requiring advanced education) can work on the assembly line to produce cars. This frees the manufacturing of cars from requiring a few skilled workers (e.g., producing a Ferrari race car largely by hand) to only requiring many relatively unskilled workers (e.g., producing a Ford model T); thus, cars can be mass produced with many unskilled workers and assembly lines as the input factors, making lower priced cars that many consumers could afford. The 2019 "Ford v Ferrari" movie provides a nice contrast between the two production modes. This was the golden age of manufacturing, when many people could find a good-paying job at a factory, because participating in the Physical Economy does not require sophisticated skill training and long-term education.

What Characterizes the Physical Economy?

We consider that there are three important characteristics of the Physical Economy: (1) human physical strength is at least somewhat important for production (in many manufacturing scenarios, physical strength is required to use machinery effectively), (2) unskilled manufacturing labor dominates, and (3) mass labor participation, but with lower average wages.

Muscle Men Dominate

For human physical strength, historian Harold James, in his 2018 "The Stupid Economy" article, says that doing physical tasks, such as farming and hunting, requires muscles, and thus humans having big muscles have a comparative advantage over the slim type.[4] We can see that human physical strength was more valuable as labor input in the Physical Economy than in the modern service economy. In those days, it was the big muscle man image that was portrayed in mass media as the "typical" worker. Figure 2.2 illustrates the muscle man in the Physical Economy on the left. Even driving a car requires more physical strength to drive a manual transmission than it does to drive an automatic transmission. The value of physical strength is even more obvious in the agriculture, forestry, fishing, and hunting sectors, which require human physical strength. Therefore, humans with physical strength (and muscle) are valued as production inputs for the Physical Economy.

Since in the Physical Economy physical strength is typically required, those people who have lower or limited physical strength are likely to be "unemployed," voluntarily or involuntarily. For example, males who have greater physical strength are employed in the agriculture sector or manufacturing sector, while females who have limited physical strength are "unemployed" at home, providing service to the household without getting paid. This gives rise to an unintended consequence of gender discrimination in the job market in the Physical Economy. In the manufacturing age, it was a male-dominated economy, because males tend to have bigger muscles and can perform such tasks easier than females. That shapes the economy to be one in which men work in factories (manufacturing) and women work at home taking care of

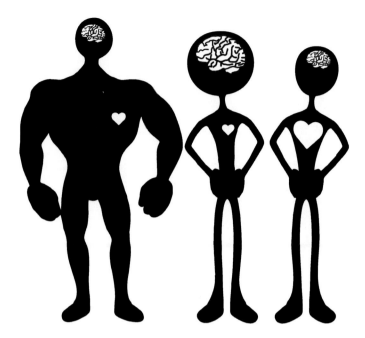

Fig. 2.2 Muscle Man, Brain Person, and Heart Woman (*Source* Authors' creation)

kids (service), a division of labor based on differences in biological, physical strengths.

Manufacturing Dominates

This is an economy in which manufacturing contributes most to the economy. Continuing the assembly line example, such production machinery greatly reduces the skill level required for manufacturing complex products (de-skilling). Thus, it is an economy in which unskilled or semi-skilled manufacturing labor dominates. It typically does not require advanced education (e.g., college degree) to work on an assembly line. Agriculture, similar to the manufacturing sector, does not typically require advanced education for skill training. However, different from the manufacturing sector, its skill acquisition hinges more on natural ability, observing others, and self-training. If we use educational level as a proxy for skill level, the two major sectors in the Physical Economy (manufacturing and farming) are both relatively unskilled, but manufacturing became the sector that contributed most to the economy.

More Opportunity for Less-Skilled Workers

This is an economy in which most humans with some basic training and education can find jobs in factories. The design of assembly lines is to break down the manufacturing process into many small, homogeneous, repetitive tasks, with each task performed by one worker. Thus, it encourages mass participation in the labor force. Although the unemployment rates tended to be lower in the Physical Economy (it was easier to find a factory job), the real wages tended to be lower than today, because the required skill level was low. Such universal labor participation means that fewer people become wealthy, but more people make a living wage. This is evocative of the communist ideology that equally poor is better than unequally rich. Worker wages and rights were protected by strong unions, which reflected the higher relative power of labor, compared to today.

Bring Manufacturing Back to the United States?

Retrospectively, the characteristics of the Physical Economy tell us the story of an economy that used machinery and many unskilled men working in factories as the inputs of production. The workers didn't make a lot of money, but most of them had a secure job; thus, it was an economy in which most of the population was happily employed.

As we are now in the Thinking Economy, in which a relatively smaller number of skilled thinking labor enjoys higher wages, while a larger number of unskilled manufacturing labor suffers from job losses and lower wages, we frequently hear politicians promising to bring manufacturing back to the United States as a means of boosting the economy. Can that be done, and is it even desirable?

To address this issue, we first need to have a better understanding about the economic arrangement of the Physical Economy. Such an economy emphasizes efficiency and quantity, not necessarily effectiveness or quality. The result is mass producing standardized commodities at an affordable price for everyone. Equality of the society is a major benefit of such an arrangement, because a majority of people in the economy can find jobs (the skill requirement is more level and typically is not high), though with somewhat lower wages. This was the time of blue-collar workers as the mainstream of the labor force.

We also need to look at this issue globally, because whether we can bring manufacturing back to the United States also depends on which countries are doing the manufacturing now. This a global division of labor issue. After the United States moved from the Physical Economy to the Thinking (service) Economy, developing countries, especially China, moved from a primitive economy to a Physical Economy that fills the manufacturing gap. This is not just happening in the United States and China. It is a global phenomenon. The global division of labor has thus become one in which developed countries use mechanical AI for manufacturing (manufacturing automation) and shift unskilled human labor to service provision, resulting in the booming of the service sector. By contrast, developing countries take advantage of their lower wages and contribute unskilled labor for manufacturing, with the help of machinery.

The transition from the Physical (manufacturing) Economy to the Thinking (service) Economy due to the rise of mechanical AI (or IT) may not always be smooth. Unskilled manufacturing workers now have difficulty finding jobs, if they do not successfully re-skill to become service labor. The global division of labor can be bumpy too, especially when developed countries still have a sufficient amount of labor that is not re-skilled (to become service labor) yet, and developing countries are eager to fill the unskilled labor gap. This is the situation that we still see with manufacturing in many places in the United States, and this has resulted in a group of unhappy, unemployed workers, because manufacturing is now automated by mechanical AI (human labor is replaced).

The US–China trade war manifests this struggle. When so much manufacturing moved to China, some of the US unskilled manufacturing labor became unemployed, because they were not yet re-skilled to become service labor. As a result, American unskilled physical workers (manufacturing and agriculture) are not happy, because their job markets have shrunk, with mechanical AI doing their jobs (manufacturing automation).

So, is it possible or desirable to bring manufacturing back to the United States? If we are talking about the manufacturing industry, yes, there is the possibility, but it will be AI doing the jobs, not unskilled human labor. The United States could eventually become a manufacturing hub again, but this time using high-tech mechanical AI that fully automates manufacturing. We have seen this all too common in what is called "Industry 4.0" being conducted with smart factories, often without any human field workers. Lauren Smiley (2019) reported in a *New York Times* AI special issue that aerial imaging companies are using high-resolution cameras and AI data analysis to aid farmers in California to control irrigation, rather than having to drive and walk endlessly to find the problem spots. Another company provides driverless tractors that can work fields around the clock, to solve the labor shortage issues.[5] These examples show that even farming will be high-tech and AI-driven. It cannot be labor-intensive, because of infeasibility (labor shortage) and/or undesirability (machines are more efficient).

Thus, to phrase the question accurately, the question at hand is whether it is possible or desirable to bring back manufacturing jobs, not the manufacturing industry (in economics, "jobs" mean human labor as the production input whereas "automation" means machines as the production input). Mechanical AI can often do such jobs much better than human labor, with greater efficiency and at lower costs. There is no way that unskilled labor in the United States can compete with unskilled labor in China (or other developing countries), given the current US wage level.

The Mechanism: Machinery Augments Unskilled Labor

The discussion of whether the United States can or should bring manufacturing back is based on the human–machine relationship in the Physical Economy. This is an economy in which machinery de-skills jobs: machinery deconstructs a complex manufacturing process into simple mechanical/physical/routine/repetitive tasks, with the result that only unskilled labor is needed for manufacturing.

In the Physical Economy, the employment and wages are more attributable to mechanical/physical/repetitive tasks, such as inspecting equipment or material, performing general physical activities, and repairing and maintaining equipment. If we look at the history, before the industrial revolution (Industry 3.0), those tasks were done by skilled human labor. With machinery and manufacturing technology, those tasks could be done by unskilled labor; thus, it appears that machinery augments unskilled labor, because more unskilled labor could participate in the production, in conjunction with *machinery automation*. We see in many developing countries, for example China, such transformation is still ongoing, with more unskilled labor moving from farming to manufacturing.

This mechanism for job change follows the process that machinery de-skills tasks, and thus allows a large number of unskilled workers to participate in routine, homogeneous manufacturing. In other words, unskilled labor is augmented by machinery (so that they are able to work along with machinery to manufacture), because machinery de-skills complex manufacturing into routine assembly lines.

The Economic Outcome: Standardization

Standardization is the major benefit (and economic output) that machinery offers in the Physical Economy. Machines are used to standardize processes so that commodities can be mass produced. This benefit is big, because it makes products available and affordable to everyone, and it encourages labor participation by lowering the skill levels required. In such an economy, people enjoy being the same as others, such as driving a Ford Model T, or watching the "I Love Lucy" TV show (even the most popular TV shows today cannot generate anywhere near the share of audience that Lucy did). For example, fast-food chain restaurant McDonalds was established around the 1940s and became very popular by offering standardized menus and foods to everyone.

Conclusions: The Future of the Physical Economy

In developed economies, the Physical Economy had its day, and that day is not coming back. Even if manufacturing returns, manufacturing jobs will not, because the tasks formerly performed by human workers will now be done by AI. Even the other pillars of the Physical Economy, farming and mining, are reinventing themselves using AI, in such a way as will minimize the need for human workers. Many of the workers displaced when the Thinking Economy pushed out the Physical Economy are still struggling, even as the *next* large displacement (from the Thinking Economy to the Feeling Economy) emerges. This creates significant societal concerns related to how to save the displaced workers. In the next chapter, we will discuss how the early forms of AI, mechanical AI, moves us further away from the Physical Economy to the Thinking Economy.

Notes

1. Huang, Ming-Hui, Roland T. Rust, and Vojislav Maksimovic (2019), "The Feeling Economy: Managing in the Next Generation of AI," *California Management Review*, 64 (4), 43–65.
2. Rust, Roland T., and Ming-Hui Huang (2014), "The Service Revolution and the Transformation of Marketing Science," *Marketing Science*, 33 (2), 206–221.
3. Association for Manufacturing Technology, https://www.amtonline.org/abo utamt/WhatisManufacturingTechnology/.

4. James, Harold (2018), "The Stupid Economy," *Project Syndicate*, January 22, https://www.project-syndicate.org/commentary/stupid-economy-declining-human-intelligence-by-harold-james-2018-01.
5. Smiley, Lauren (2019), "Eyes in the Sky Aid Farmers on the Ground," *The New York Times*, Artificial Intelligence issue. September 18.

3

The Thinking Economy

As physical labor became automated, human physical labor became devalued. This created a Thinking Economy, in which the most valued human skill was thinking. We still mostly live in the Thinking Economy, but there are starting to be cracks. AI is beginning to make impressive inroads in thinking, which is now threatening the economic value of human thinking. We explore in this chapter the nature of the Thinking Economy, AI's progress in thinking, and consider what this means for human labor.

In 1997, IBM's Deep Blue defeated the world chess champion Garry Kasparov. It played like a human, by learning from chess grandmasters' strategies (a cognitive reasoning approach to learning). In 2017 (almost 20 years later), Google's AlphaGo Zero beat China's Ke Jie, the number one Go player in the world. This time, AlphaGo Zero played like a machine, by playing countless games against itself and finding out the ways to win (a data mapping approach to learning).

The main difference between the games of chess and Go is that in each turn, the possible moves for chess (about 35) is much less than Go (about 250), and a good chess player can remember the history of his own and his opponent's moves and come up with reactive moves accordingly. This is the human's way to learn: know the problem (i.e., remember the previous moves and understand the current situation) and react accordingly (i.e., figuring out how to move next). Deep Blue is a computer that employs human-like strategies, but with super computing power. It is more like a human with super computing power (i.e., Deep Blue) playing against a human without super computing power (i.e., Garry Kasparov). That is no insult to Kasparov, whose own innate human computing power is impressive!

© The Author(s) 2021
R. T. Rust and M.-H. Huang, *The Feeling Economy*,
https://doi.org/10.1007/978-3-030-52977-2_3

By contrast to chess, the possible moves for Go are almost unlimited, i.e., approaching infinity, and thus a good memory is not enough. Computer Go AI software does not remember all possible moves, but rather learns based on reinforcement learning, such that a winning move is reinforced, and a losing move is punished. Over time, machines learn how to win, even if they don't understand why. In this way of learning, machines do not know why a certain move is winning, but it learns that such a move is more likely to lead to winning.

As AI becomes better at thinking, how will the Thinking Economy change? We will show that some types of thinking will be valuable longer than others.

In the Thinking Economy, employment and wages are more attributable to thinking tasks, such as processing, analyzing and interpreting information, planning and prioritizing work, making decisions, and solving problems. The technological driving force of the Thinking Economy is information technology (IT), machines that store, retrieve, transmit, and manipulate data or information.

We discussed in Chapter 2 how machinery and manufacturing technology gave rise to the Physical Economy by de-skilling tasks and allowing unskilled humans to enjoy labor market participation. With the continuing advancement of technology, from physical/mechanical technology to information technology, we enter the Thinking Economy, in which machines can often do mechanical jobs alone, with data input. We call such machines mechanical AI (employing information technology), which can learn or adapt at most minimally.

Mechanical AI can learn and adapt from data. However, as discussed earlier, learning is not always central to its role, either because it is unnecessary or because it is undesirable. With mechanical AI, the repetitive manufacturing jobs can often be done totally by machine. Human unskilled manufacturing labor is no longer needed. Displaced workers either need to move to the service sector (re-skilling) or upgrade their skills (up-skilling).

To understand how mechanical AI drives the Thinking Economy, and what the nature of the Thinking Economy is, we first discuss two types of thinking intelligence to illustrate the comparative strength of humans vs. machines, and then discuss how our current skill training and education facilitate the "single" thinking intelligence view. This view was famously challenged when Daniel Goleman published his "Emotional Intelligence: Why It Can Matter More Than IQ" book in 1996.[1] Our multiple intelligences view also shows that there are multiple intelligences for both humans and machines (since the latter is designed to mimic human intelligences).

Characteristics of AI

There are two defining characteristics of AI: self-learning and network connectivity. The two characteristics apply to all of the AI intelligences discussed in this book.

Self-Learning

For any technology to be considered intelligent, it must be able to learn from data and adapt over time. In this sense, mechanical AI is more advanced than simpler machinery, due to its capability to learn from data. This is what distinguishes information technology (i.e., mechanical AI) from earlier machinery, with mechanical AI having information processing capability that earlier machinery lacked. The ability to learn from data and update outcomes is what makes a machine intelligent.

Based on this defining characteristic, to be qualified as mechanical AI, it needs to have the capability to learn and adapt, even if it only has very limited data and learning capability or does not learn all the time. For example, a computer or a cellphone that is designed to provide only a prescribed set of functions is not AI, due to limited ability to learn. The reasons to design AI as mechanical can be for necessity (i.e., nothing new to learn) or desirability (i.e., generating consistent output), as discussed in Chapter 2.

Network Connectivity

If we say that the technology backbone of the Thinking Economy (i.e., computerization of manufacturing) is information technology, then the technology backbone of the Feeling Economy (i.e., digitization of manufacturing) is digital networking. (These roughly correspond to what has been referred to as Industry 3.0 and Industry 4.0.) In a digitally networked system, computers are connected, and communicate with one another. Machines are not stand-alone anymore; instead, they learn from each other. If one machine makes a mistake, all other machines in the network learn from that mistake and can avoid it. Network connectivity is the key driving force for the evolution from Industry 3.0 to 4.0. In Industry 4.0, digital networking automates and optimizes the entire system. In this fourth industrial revolution, smart and autonomous systems, fueled by data and machine learning, often are able to operate autonomously, even for complex products (replacing skilled labor).

AI is inherently networked. In the digital, social age, it is even difficult to come up with any digital technologies that are not able to connect to the Internet and/or with each other. Network connectivity scales up AI's learning by making data in the digital network ubiquitously available. For example, autonomous cars use swarm intelligence to learn about driving and road conditions from all other autonomous cars that are also connected to the Internet of Things (IoT) network.

Ability to Adapt

Mechanical AI can learn from data and can potentially be networked. As long as machines can learn and adapt, they are AI. It is their learning and adaptive capability that drive the economy into a Thinking one. Machinery augments unskilled humans to do tasks that formerly required skilled labor, such as manufacturing cars. In contrast, mechanical AI (e.g., computer and IT) replaces unskilled labor in the assembly lines, because by learning from data, they can assemble cars on their own (manufacturing automation).

The Forms of Mechanical AI

When talking about mechanical AI, the images of various embodied robots often pop up, probably due to their anthropomorphic appearance. In fact, mechanical AI is more likely to be embedded machines, i.e., they do not have a physical appearance like robots, but operate at the back end, such as apps. Even if they are embodied, they are more likely to be just machine arms, rather than the humanoid robots depicted in the sci-fi movies. All levels of AI can be designed to be embodied or embedded.

Embodied Robots

When machines are designed to have a physical body, they are embodied, and the term "robots" is often applied (although the term is also applied to embedded machines, such as chatbots).

Embodied robots vary in how human-like they look. They can be designed to look like interactive kiosks, or they can be designed to look like humans, as humanoid or anthropomorphic robots. Machine arms in factory just look like machinery (even if we call them "arms"), ATM machines are stand-alone robotic big boxes; Marty, the robots used in Giant Food Stores, are tall, weird machines with big googly eyes for observing in-store conditions; social robots, e.g., SoftBank's Pepper, are cute little guys that look half-machine and half-human, ASUS's Zenbo, looks more like 2/3 machine and 1/3 human, and check-in robotic staff at the Henn na Hotel in Japan look almost as real as human staff.

Why do we sometimes design machines to look like machines but sometimes to look like humans? What are the considerations? One simple rule of thumb for designing mechanical robots (we will revisit this robot design issue in Chapter 14, AI for Feeling) is that if the machines are used to interact with humans physically, they are more likely to be designed to have some human characteristics. For example, the social robot, Pepper, is designed to look like humans, but is still discernable from humans, and is used to interact with human consumers directly. Its human appearance is to make human consumers feel like they are interacting with a human, and the machine appearance is to make human consumers know that they are still interacting with machines. Some studies show that consumers are open to humanoid robots, but some studies show the opposite. The general conclusion is that it is better to design humanoid robots to be discernable from humans, otherwise human consumers may experience an eerie phenomenon called the "uncanny valley," in which humans find robots that look like humans to be creepy if their appearance is a little bit "too close for comfort." That's why SoftBank and ASUS design their social robots to look like humans to different degrees. We also see that an easy way out is to design social robots to look like cute pets, such as ASUS's Zenbo, to avoid the uncanny valley.

Humanoid embodied robots are more difficult and costly to develop, because of the additional hardware requirements to make them act and react like humans to carry out natural social interactions. In the front end, they need to be equipped with camera, microphone, and sensors, to capture a consumer's physical activity state; for example, whether the consumer is walking, how fast he is walking, and whether he is walking toward or away from the robot, and in the back end they need to have the networking, data storage, and analytics capabilities to access, collect, and analyze the personal data and social background of the consumers they are interacting with to act and react in real time. Such eye–hand–foot coordination and finger dexterity are still difficult for machines to achieve. Thus, we see commercial robots such as Kuri, Pepper, AIBO, and Jibo robots, but none of them can be relied on to take over most household chores.

Alternatively, embodied robots do not need to look like humans, if their functions are not to physically interact with humans. For example, hotel housekeeping service robots do not need to look like humans, because they perform back-end mechanical tasks such as making the bed and vacuuming the floor, rather than chatting with customers interactively. Roomba is simply a round-shaped mopping robot for vacuum cleaning. There is no need to design it to look like a human house cleaner. With the recent coronavirus spread, delivery bots have become a popular option. When we are advised against human contact, even food delivery is not safe, if the food is delivered by humans (because we still need to open the door, get the food from the delivery person, and sometimes sign and pay). Kiwi Campus, a start-up near Berkeley campus, uses more than 60,000 robotic food deliveries (about the size of a breadbasket, equipped with an onboard computer and six cameras) to deliver foods. Customers' reactions are positive, because they believe robotic delivery is more hygienic than people-based food deliveries.

Embedded Machines

Most mechanical AI are embedded machines, i.e., they do not have a physical appearance like embodied robots, but operate at the back end, as applications. Virtual personal assistants and chatbots are common embedded machines. Consumers use virtual personal assistants, such as Amazon Alexa and Google Home to handle their daily life routines, without the need to use the mouse, keyboard, and screen of their devices anymore. One can ask Alexa any simple question orally and then Alexa will search the Internet for answers. One can also command Google Home to switch off the lights at home remotely. These personal assistants do not have a human body, and take care of daily routines for consumers, so that consumers can focus their attention on things that are more important.

Many service providers also automate their service offerings and processes using various embedded mechanical AI applications without physical visibility, such as online banking (money withdrawing, depositing, and transferring, not financial planning), online customer service, or virtual personal assistants. Online customer service uses embedded machines extensively. For example, at the mechanical level, there are text-based chatbots, in which customers interact with machines using text. This is more like a mechanical AI version of telephone customer service, with customers interacting with the chatbot agents using text rather than voice. Such text-based mechanical chatbots are very efficient; they can handle a large number of customers' routine questions at the same time. There is no need for them to have a physical appearance. Often, companies still put a human picture (often a woman) on the website to make customers feel that they are chatting with a human agent. Such chatbots can also be audio-based, that is, they can carry out human-like conversations with customers. We consider the audio-based chatbots to be feeling AI, because it requires more advanced machine learning to implement, which will be discussed in Chapter 14, AI for Feeling.

Mechanical AI: Replacement and Augmentation

Machines can be humans' friends or enemies. Although they are always invented to augment humans (make humans more capable or reduce humans' efforts), once the machines outperform humans, there may be no need to keep humans in the loop. Mechanical AI, with the capability to learn and adapt, and the capability to learn from other connected machines, can automate manufacturing without the participation of unskilled human labor. This is sometimes called Industry 3.0, in which manufacturing automation is achieved by *computerization*.

In the Thinking Economy, we can see that machines replace as well as augment humans. On one hand, mechanical AI replaces unskilled manufacturing labor, forcing workers to shift to the service sector (re-skilling). In modern smart factories, there is little human labor in assembly lines, replaced by machine arms, because manufacturing is fully automated. Mechanical AI has the relative advantage over unskilled human labor of being extremely consistent (e.g., free from human fatigue or variation) and productive (i.e., a few machines can generate a huge amount of output, and turn a two-factor productivity input [labor and machine] into one-factor productivity [machine only]).

On the other hand, mechanical AI augments thinking labor by taking care of routine, repetitive, administrative tasks, so that humans can concentrate on thinking (up-skilling). When mechanical AI takes care of the "doing" jobs, humans emphasize thinking. Human labor moves from factories to offices, and the economy transforms from manufacturing to service. It is this duality (replacing manufacturing labor and augmenting thinking labor) that often causes debates about whether machines replace or augment humans.

Economists like Autor and Dorn observe that computerization (i.e., mechanical AI) polarizes the US labor market by pushing unskilled manufacturing labor into unskilled service jobs.[2] In other words, mechanical AI sets the foundation for the service economy. The Thinking Economy is a service one by nature. It is not based on manufacturing commodities, but rather is based on providing heterogeneous intangible service. Many companies have gone through this service transformation due to computerization. In our 2014 article in the journal, *Marketing Science*, we point out that the advance of information technologies, such as big data, cloud computing, and mobile communication make customer data ubiquitously available, allowing better and more personalized service that eventually results in the expansion of service in the economy.[3]

How would mechanical AI transform our economy, from Physical to Thinking? We consider that in general mechanical AI replaces unskilled manufacturing labor but augments skilled service labor. We elaborate our prediction below. Figure 3.1 illustrates this mechanism.

Replace Unskilled Manufacturing Labor

Replacement in the Thinking Economy occurs when mechanical AI is used to automate unskilled manufacturing jobs. In this scenario, we can find smart factories having no field workers, and an entire assembly line automated using mechanical AI. This is the situation in which machines replace humans as an economic input; that is, unskilled labor shrinks and capital increases, for reasons of productivity. Those displaced unskilled manufacturing workers can (1) become unemployed, which causes an unemployment problem in the society, (2) re-skill to become unskilled service labor, for example to become waiter/waitress or office secretary,[4] (3) up-skill to become skilled manufacturing labor, for example get a STEM education and become an engineer, or (4) up-skill and/or re-skill to become skilled service labor. From options 1–4, the difficulty of attainment increases, as up-skilling requires longer training and advanced education, which is a barrier to many unskilled manufacturing workers. Path 3 is slightly easier, but may not have as much potential as option 4, because thinking machines will soon be able to replace such jobs as well (to be discussed in Chapter 4, the Feeling Economy). As a result, most unskilled manufacturing labor becomes unskilled service labor, as Autor and Dorn documented.

Augment Skilled Service Labor

Augmentation in the Thinking Economy can occur when mechanical AI is used to automate unskilled service jobs, such as administration. When more unskilled service jobs are filled by either unskilled manufacturing labor (those contextual service tasks such as restaurant waiting) or mechanical AI (those routine and repetitive tasks such as withdrawing cash from ATM, using self-check-in, or getting information from a kiosk), unskilled service

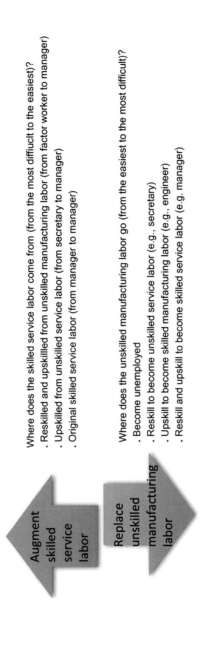

Where does the skilled service labor come from (from the most diffiuclt to the easiest)?
. Reskilled and upskilled from unskilled manufacturing labor (from factor worker to manager)
. Upskilled from unskilled service labor (from secretary to manager)
. Original skilled service labor (from manager to manager)

Where does the unskilled manufacturing labor go (from the easiest to the most difficult)?
. Become unemployed
. Reskill to become unskilled service labor (e.g., secretary)
. Upskill to become skilled manufacturing labor (e.g., engineer)
. Reskill and upskill to become skilled service labor (e.g. manager)

Augment skilled service labor

Replace unskilled manufacturing labor

Fig. 3.1 The dual mechanism of mechanical AI on labor (*Source* Authors' creation)

workers need to upgrade their skills to become skilled service labor (up-skilling). Not all services are heavily context-dependent and heterogeneous. Many routine, repetitive service tasks can be performed by mechanical AI, such as hotel check-in kiosks, housekeeping, vacuum cleaning, and administrative tasks in an office. When these routine, repetitive service tasks can be done by machines, unskilled service workers (e.g., secretaries) need to up-skill to become skilled service workers (e.g., managers). Such skilled service labor can be augmented by mechanical AI (e.g., secretary's tasks are automated, e.g., managers use Google Calendar to plan daily events) to concentrate on higher-level thinking and feeling tasks. Of course, those who are skilled service workers to begin with can be similarly augmented by mechanical AI to make themselves more productive.

Together, this dual mechanism of augmentation and replacement replaces unskilled manufacturing labor and augments skilled service labor, giving rise to the Thinking Economy.

What Characterizes the Thinking Economy?

If we say that the Physical Economy is the past (at least for developed economies), then the Thinking Economy is the present. We are in the Thinking Economy, in which humans do the thinking, because machines do the doing. The Thinking Economy is characterized by: (1) "brain person" (now often women, as well as men) having a comparative advantage over "muscle man," (2) service provision and consumption dominate the economy, (3) the income distribution tends to be less equal, but the average wages tend to be higher, because skilled service labor requires higher education to attain the necessary skill set, but not everyone has the ability or opportunity to achieve it, and (4) STEM jobs are preferred to less-skilled jobs, because they ensure good pay.

Brain Person Dominates

In contrast to the "muscle man" in the Physical Economy, in the Thinking Economy, the human brain (not muscles) is valued most as an economic input. This also has an impact on human body shape. When physical strength is no longer valued as economic input, brain people are often stereotyped as skinny computer geeks, due to the reduced demand for human muscle.[5] The *New York Times* even reports about the battle of brains and brawn, such that when both muscles and minds are stressed, i.e., thinking hard while working out, brains tend to trump brawn.[6] The decreased emphasis on physical strength means that women can now compete on a more or less equal basis, resulting in huge gains for women. These gains for women will accelerate further in the Feeling Economy, as we discuss in Chapter 7. Figure 2.2 in Chapter 2 illustrates this brain person in the middle having a skinny body, small heart, but a big brain.

Service Dominates

In the Thinking Economy, the service sector is the most important part of the economy. Service jobs are white-collar, indoor office, thinking jobs. The twofold mechanism discussed earlier expands the thinking (service) economy. It creates the service polarization phenomenon documented in Autor and Dorn, i.e., the growth of unskilled service labor employment due to unskilled manufacturing workers becoming unskilled service workers, and mechanical AI doing the unskilled service tasks that augment skilled service jobs. Both the unskilled and skilled parts of the service sector are expanded, resulting in the polarization (bimodal distribution) of service employment. As a result, service labor (both unskilled and skilled) dominates the Thinking Economy. What Autor and Dorn did not observe is that the unskilled service sector does not grow evenly. It is the contextual unskilled service jobs that are growing. The non-contextual unskilled service jobs can be automated with mechanical AI, a prediction made based on our theory.

Inequality of Wealth

Human thinking intelligence does not always come naturally. It often requires long years of training and advanced education. This contrasts with machinery that enabled the mass labor market participation of unskilled manufacturing workers. In the Physical Economy, most men, even those less-skilled, could find jobs at factories. In the Thinking Economy, advanced education is rewarded with a wage premium, and fewer people (compared with the scenario in the Physical Economy where most people can find a factory job) can succeed in this up-skilling career path. Thus, the income distribution is less equal, with skilled thinking workers making much more money than unskilled manufacturing and thinking workers. Assuming that the number of unskilled thinking workers is larger than the number of skilled thinking workers, we can expect an economy with more income inequality.

STEM Jobs Rule

In the Thinking Economy, science education is rewarded with a wage premium, and the wage premium, in turn, motivates people to major in STEM subjects, such as engineering, computer science, or mathematics. This results in the dominance of science education in higher education. In some Asian cultures, the term "Tiger parenting" or "Tiger mom" describes authoritarian parents striving hard to provide resources for educating their kids to be successful in their careers, mostly in "hard" science such as computer science and engineering, because those jobs earn high pay. If kids pursue a "soft" science major, such as arts and humanity, they often have to fight with their ambitious parents, because those majors are considered to lead to lower-paying jobs, if jobs can be found at all. In the United States, the dominance of STEM (science, technology, engineering, and mathematics) education reflects the same thought—in the Thinking Economy, science ensures good pay.

Can Machines Take Thinking Jobs Away from Humans?

Humans currently do well with thinking jobs, but do they have to worry about losing those to AI? There are bipolar views. Those who are pessimistic think machines can take over even thinking jobs from humans. In our 2018 *Journal of Service Research* article on AI in Service, we propose a replacement scenario, using analytical modeling to show that as machine intelligences advance from mechanical, to analytical, to intuitive, to empathetic, machines will assume more jobs, in the order that mechanical labor is first replaced, followed by thinking labor, and eventually even empathetic labor might be replaced by true emotional machines (i.e., machines that can feel).[7] We will discuss this in Chapter 14, AI for Feeling. In the singularity, there may be no jobs remaining for humans to do. In the worst case, there may be no humans left at all, since machines would be superior to humans in all intelligences, making humans obsolete. We discuss these scenarios in more detail in Chapter 15.

Those who are optimistic think machines are invented to help humans; thus, machines will never be able to replace humans. Augmentation has been discussed extensively in the literature, because this is what humans prefer to believe. It reflects the optimistic view about machines, but it is also a perhaps myopic and parochial human-centric view: machines cannot be better than humans. Various possibilities are laid out for machines to help humans become better humans. For example, Thomas Malone says that machines can be (1) physical tools like a hammer or a lawn mower, (2) assistants, like a human assistant, helping to get things done, (3) peers, like a co-worker, and (4) managers, like human managers, telling us what to do.[8] Thomas Davenport and Julia Kirby tell us to step up (e.g., be a brand manager), step aside (e.g., be a creative), step in (e.g., be a pricing expert), step narrowly (e.g., be a "wrap advertising" specialist), or step forward (e.g., be a digital innovator) so that we can add value to ourselves to go beyond automation.[9] These are great suggestions from big thinkers.

Just as machinery augmented unskilled workers in factories and made manufacturing more productive, mechanical AI (i.e., using information technology) can augment human thinking (skilled service labor), as discussed previously. The observation that both machinery and IT augment humans makes people believe that regardless of what kind of machines, humans, unskilled and skilled, will continue to be augmented. Various theories have been proposed to reinforce this rosy belief. In the information systems literature, we can see that decision support systems is one major research stream that studies how information technology can be used in various situations to support human decisions. However, this rosy picture may not continue with AI, because AI is characterized by self-learning and network connectivity. When AI can learn and adapt over time, and when AI is not just stand-alone machines (meaning that they have collective intelligence, learning from each other), assuming AI will always be subservient to humans might be unrealistic. Bear in mind that mechanical AI is designed to have limited learning capability. When AI advances to the thinking level, as it is in the process of doing today, the rosy picture of believing AI will help humans think even more wisely may not hold.

To address this issue, we need to go back to our original four intelligences view, published in the *Journal of Service Research* in 2018, in which we distinguish two types of thinking intelligence.

Analytical Intelligence

This is the basic level of thinking intelligence. Analytical AI learns or adapts systematically mainly based on "big" data. This is the dominant AI in the current Thinking Economy, with machine learning as the major approach to learning. Anything that can be programmed can be learned. Analytical AI is not extremely smart, from the standpoint of common sense or intuition, but the huge computing power at an affordable cost makes it super powerful in analyzing data far beyond what human brains can process. We see that

AI can win at chess or quiz shows, even defeating human champions. Those games are rule-based, have a finite number of possible moves (even though the number of possibilities is extremely high, far beyond what a human's brain can handle), and thus can be handled easily by analytical AI with the right data input.

Intuitive Intelligence

This is the advanced level of thinking intelligence, and is the intermediate level between thinking and feeling (i.e., empathetic) AI. It learns and adapts based on understanding. The word "understanding" is used here to refer to learning from limited data (i.e., "small" data), such as common sense or intuition. As common sense or intuition are not rule-based, they are much more difficult to program. Machine learning, currently the major method for analytical AI, may be too "mechanical" for intuitive intelligence. The game of Go, discussed at the opening, is closer to this thinking level. This is the level of AI intelligence to which many computer scientists currently devote their efforts. The goal is to develop AI that has the capability to do common-sense reasoning.[10] To achieve this, AI needs to be able to apply knowledge (as opposed to just analyze data) to solve new problems that it has never encountered before. "Understanding" in this sense thus also means that AI needs to possess "knowledge" to understand novel situations. Humans and machines each have their strengths on the two types of thinking intelligence. Currently, machines are good at calculative and analytical thinking, whereas humans are good at intuition and common sense. For the two types of thinking intelligence, we are pessimistic about humans' outlook to outperform analytical AI, with all the evidence pointing to the conclusion that analytical AI will only be more powerful over time, with computing power continuing to increase and computing costs continuing to decrease. While being pessimistic about analytical AI, we are more optimistic that humans will be able to outperform machines with respect to intuitive intelligence for a longer time. Advancing from analytical to intuitive intelligence is not linear, and intuitive intelligence may not be achievable with the current machine learning approach to AI intelligence.

The Economic Outcome: Personalization

Personalization is the major benefit (and driver of economic output) of the Thinking Economy. In contrast to standardization in the Physical Economy, personalization means offering different things to different consumers based on their different preferences. The assumption is that every consumer's preference is different, and the consumer likes to be treated as an individual. This is very different from the mass production, mass media age of the Physical Economy. People no longer enjoy being the same and consuming the same thing (at least they do not treat such consumption as a luxury); instead, the new philosophy is to be unique, like Apple computer's famous slogan "be different."

The benefit of personalization has long been recognized in the twentieth century, but we don't have the means and resources to achieve total personalization, due to the high costs involved in it. For example, if every customer had her own brand, it would be a wonderful thing, but the cost of advertising so many brands would be exorbitant. The high costs can be due to the difficulty of identifying each consumer's preference or the difficulty of offering individually different products. In the service economy, the latter becomes less an issue, because service is, by nature, different across consumers. The former difficulty is resolved by analytical AI. The major driving force is analytical AI that is very good at recognizing patterns and categorizing things from big data. The data can be text, image, or audio. Remember the dual mechanism that mechanical AI replaces unskilled manufacturing labor and augments skilled service labor. The role of analytical AI is further away from replacing unskilled manufacturing labor and has more to do with augmenting skilled service labor. For example, managers' jobs can be augmented by both mechanical AI and analytical AI. Mechanical AI automates daily routine planning (e.g., Google Calendar) and analytical AI provides analytics output as the basis of the managers' strategic decisions.

Given the power of analytical AI in pattern recognition, personalization becomes its major benefit. For example, Netflix relies on machine learning to recommend movies to its customers. Such a personalization involves two systems of machine learning: one system analyzes the movie watching pattern (what type of movies the consumer likes and dislikes), and one system comes up with the recommended movies (what to recommend to the consumer). In the Thinking Economy, almost everything can be personalized, based on big data input and machine learning algorithms and models. When we go to Amazon.com, it always recognizes us immediately, either because we sign in (it will prompt us to sign into see personalized recommendations) or based on our browsing behavior on the website, and then we will see a list of recommended products like "other people who see (purchase) this product also see (purchase) those products…"

Conclusions

How can humans survive and thrive in the Thinking Economy? In other words, what is humans' differential advantage over AI? AI seems certain to assume an increasing percentage of analytical thinking tasks, but humans may be able to hold off AI (for a while), with respect to intuitive thinking tasks. By distinguishing the two types of thinking intelligences, we have a clearer picture of what machines good at. Current machines are powerhouses of analytical thinking; thus, as humans we should not compete head-to-head against it (think of those vanquished chess and Go champions) by striving to think like a computer. Nevertheless, current machines are still not good at intuitive thinking; thus, we can enjoy thinking intuitively (even not 100% rationally), and refer to data analytics to support our intuitions. When analytical thinking is automated by machines, humans should emphasize intuitive thinking.

Notes

1. Goleman, Daniel (1996), *Emotional Intelligence: Why It Can Matter More than IQ*, Bloomsbury Publishing.
2. Autor, David H., and David Dorn (2013), "The Growth of Low-Skill Service Jobs and the Polarization of the US Labor Market," *American Economic Review*, 103 (5), 1553–1597.
3. Rust, Roland T., and Ming-Hui Huang (2014), "The Service Revolution and the Transformation of Marketing Science," *Marketing Science*, 33 (2), 206–221.
4. Re-skilling is to acquire a different set of skills without involving advancing skills to a higher level. For example, from an unskilled manufacturing labor to an unskilled service labor.
5. James, Harold (2018), "The Stupid Economy," *Project Syndicate*, January 22, https://www.project-syndicate.org/commentary/stupid-economy-declining-human-intelligence-by-harold-james-2018-01.
6. Reynolds, Gretchen (2017), "The Battle of Brains vs. Brawn," *The New York Times*, October 25, https://www.nytimes.com/2017/10/25/well/move/the-battle-of-brains-vs-brawn.html.
7. Huang, Ming-Hui, and Roland T. Rust (2018), "Artificial Intelligence in Service," *Journal of Service Research*, 21 (2), 155–172.
8. Malone, Thomas W. (2018), "How Human-Computer 'Superminds' Are Redefining the Future of Work," *MIT Sloan Management Review*, 59 (40), 34–41.
9. Davenport, Thomas H., and Julia Kirby (2015), "Beyond Automation," *Harvard Business Review*, June, 59–65.

10. Davis, Ernest, and Gary Marcus (2015), "Commonsense Reasoning and Commonsense Knowledge in Artificial Intelligence," *Communications of the ACM*, 58 (9), 93–103.

4

The Feeling Economy

As AI assumes an increasing number of thinking tasks, eventually including even intuitive thinking tasks, humans will find that their highest and best use involves emotion, empathy, and interpersonal relationships. At that point, we will be in a Feeling Economy, in which AI specializes in thinking, and humans specialize in feeling. We are not there yet, but the trend is already clear, and supported by empirical data. We project, based on the current rate of change, that feeling tasks should be more important than thinking tasks for human workers by the year 2036.

Feeling is biological, and is not limited to humans. Dogs (lovers of other pets can change the pet type to any species of their preference) have feelings and are very pleasant for their owners to be with, even though they only have the thinking intelligence of a human two-year-old. Babies don't have to learn to cry when they are hungry and smile when they see their mother. For biological beings, feelings come naturally, without conscious learning. Only when we grow up, we learn to regulate our emotions, because some emotions may be inappropriate for some situations (e.g., it is impolite to show boring expressions in a classroom) or when the consequences of the emotions may be bad (being angry at other drivers on the road may cause ourselves to drive badly too, or in extreme cases even result in confrontation).

Machines, on the other hand, do not have natural feelings. Understanding emotions, and forming an emotional response is very difficult for AI, even though it is an active topic of research. Someday, machines will likely become sufficiently feeling intelligent that even emotions will not be a lasting advantage for humans. We will discuss this eventuality in Chapters 14 and 15. Meanwhile, however, there will be a period of time, probably decades, in

© The Author(s) 2021
R. T. Rust and M.-H. Huang, *The Feeling Economy*,
https://doi.org/10.1007/978-3-030-52977-2_4

which humans' best hope is to become really good at feeling intelligence and interpersonal relationships. This chapter explains the basis for the Feeling Economy, and its implications for human society.

Biological vs. Machine Intelligences

The introduction to this chapter highlights the differences between biological beings and artificial beings. Only biological beings have biological intelligence, which includes the ability to think intuitively and feel biologically, because of their brain, heart, and nervous system that link together the laws of physics and chemistry. When we feel angry, our face appears grouchy (facial expression), our heart rate increases (biological reaction), and we are inclined to do something to remove the cause of the bad feeling (behavior); all of these are wired by our nervous and chemical systems.

Biological intelligences are demonstrated by humans and other animals, and are associated with physiological reactions to external stimuli, to adapt to the environment. Neuroscience is one such discipline that studies the structure and function of the nervous system that is unique to biological beings.[1]

Animal psychologists try to compare animal intelligences with human intelligences, and conclude that even when nonhuman animals demonstrate human-like intelligent behaviors, those animals may not always be considered as intelligent, because the way they learn the behaviors can be different from human learning.[2] Some famous psychological principles have been experimentally established by animal psychologists, such as Pavlov's classical conditioning learning[3] and Skinner's operant conditioning learning,[4] about how animals learn certain behaviors based on their positive and negative emotions (approach or avoidance behavior).

What Is the Feeling Economy?

The distinction between biological beings and artificial beings illustrates that machines cannot experience emotions in a biological manner. We do not mean that machines cannot have or show emotions in a machine way. We have seen various applications of machines interacting with humans emotionally, such as chatbots for customer service, and conversational bots to mimic human conversations. Replika, a machine learning-based chatbot, provides emotional comfort to consumers by mimicking their styles of communication. After a couple of months' training, the consumer often feels that the chatbot really understands every bit of his feeling (i.e., the machine seemingly demonstrates empathic capability). The machine learning approach that Replika uses does not understand the consumer's emotions, but simply "replicates" the consumer's way of communication. After training, the consumer actually is talking to himself in his own way. The more the consumer opens up to the chatbot, the closer the chatbot can match the consumer's communication style. However, these applications are about machines "showing" human-like EQ, but not "experiencing" human emotions.

The biology mostly limits machines today to the thinking intelligence realm. The continuing advancement of thinking AI, from analytical to intuitive, further limits any human advantage in thinking. Machines will not stop their development at analytical thinking. When machines are capable of intuitive thinking, human workers will have to move to feeling tasks, because biological-based intelligence is what will be left for them. Thus, thinking AI gives rise to the emergence of the Feeling Economy. The capability of AI is currently expanding beyond mechanical to analytical thinking, and eventually even to intuitive thinking. When AI performs many of the thinking tasks, human workers will gravitate more toward interpersonal and empathetic tasks. This is the main reason for the emergence of the Feeling Economy.

The Feeling Economy is an economy in which human employment and wages are more attributable to feeling tasks and jobs. Feeling/empathetic tasks are the "soft" aspects of a job, for example, communicating with people, establishing and maintaining relationships, and influencing others. Doing these tasks well requires human workers to have good EQ and good soft, social, and people skills. Those people skills are not highly valued in the Thinking Economy, compared with hard skills. It is a "soft" service economy, compared with the "hard" service Thinking Economy (e.g., engineers), and service jobs emphasizing those soft skills will be booming (e.g., marketers).

The Feeling Economy is characterized by humans doing the feeling tasks and machines doing the thinking tasks. This may upend the current social order. For example, groups that currently dominate in the Thinking Economy (e.g., white people, Asians) may find that their advantage declines in the Feeling Economy. Some traditionally less-advantaged people (e.g., ethnic minorities, women) may find that they are no longer disadvantaged in the Feeling Economy, and some groups (e.g., women) may achieve a significantly higher status, as we will show in Chapter 7.

How Do Machines Think?

When machines can do all sorts of thinking (analytical and intuitive) better than humans, humans should relinquish the thinking tasks to them. We have introduced the two levels of machine thinking intelligence—analytical and intuitive—in Chapter 3, the Thinking Economy. Currently machines are advancing rapidly toward intuitive thinking, which has important implications for how soon the Feeling Economy will arrive. Actually, the Feeling Economy will arrive gradually, and empirical research indicates that the process is already well underway.

The key to achieving intuitive AI intelligence is how machines can learn to think. There is a human way and a machine way to thinking intelligence. Computer scientists have tried, and are still trying, to design machines that can think in the human way, but so far it is not very successful. Instead, currently machines are designed to think in a machine way. So far, we have no conclusion as to which way is better and whether machines can be designed to think in the human way or not. When machines are designed to think in a machine way, this is the "machine learning" approach to intelligence (illustrated by the Replika case), while when machines are designed to think in the human way, this is the "reasoning" approach to intelligence. We introduce the two methods of learning below.

Mapping Approach

The mapping approach is the method used by modern machine learning. It designs machines to answer questions without knowing how they achieve their answers, or even any ability to explain them. Sound weird? But it's true. Most modern machine learning uses neural networks (computing systems that mimic biological neural networks) to map and categorize input data into output patterns. In this process, machines do not need to have knowledge to answer questions, but simply with big data, great computing power, and the right algorithms and models, the mapping mechanism can be very powerful in generating output that is seemingly intelligent. For example, AlphaGo plays the Go game in a way that is distinct from the way the human champion plays, by learning from countless past games, and coming up with the strategies that have the highest chance to win. It does not know why these strategies win in a certain situation. A notable real-world example was that in 2015 the Allen Institute for AI hosted a global competition for designing AI to answer eighth-grade multiple-choice science questions. Those questions covered a broad range of knowledge domains, but all had the standard four responses. None of the top three winners trained their machines to understand the questions (in a human intelligence sense); instead, they used various information-retrieval methods to predict the likelihood of the right answers. The top prize winner combined 15 models based on properties of the questions (e.g., length of question, form of answer, and relationships among answer options). The second-place team scored question-answer similarity, and the third-place team transformed answer choices A, B, C, and D to all possible pairs.[5]

This approach to thinking intelligence results in the famous Turing test, such that it doesn't matter how machines think, as long as the outcomes appear to be as intelligent as human outcomes. The intelligence demonstrated is at the analytical level, not the intuitive level. Situations that are outside the range of the data used to learn may be badly mishandled. For example, many AI models that are based on the machine learning approach are struggling in the era of the coronavirus pandemic, because the situation is unprecedented.

Reasoning Approach

The reasoning approach tries to design machines that have knowledge, and can apply the knowledge to answer questions (i.e., reasoning). This is the human way of thinking. This way of learning is important for responding to unknown and new environments. We don't just learn from histories; we also need to learn from intuition and common sense.

Expert systems in the early days were applications that tried to represent and use expert knowledge in computer systems. However, this approach underperformed, relative to expectations, resulting in several "AI winters" in the early days of AI research and applications (meaning the funding and resources for this approach to learning were mostly withdrawn or discontinued), due to the bottleneck of designing machines to do cognitive reasoning, according to computer scientist Adnan Darwiche.[6] This approach, if eventually successful, can be expected to lead to intuitive machine intelligence, such that machines can address the "why" issue, not just the "what" issue so that learned knowledge can be applied to new situations, and can learn in a holistic manner (i.e., intuition and commonsense) to solve general problems (i.e., strong AI, AI that has the full spectrum of human intelligence), not just by mapping input data to output data (i.e., narrow AI, AI that is very good at a specific task); and can "experience" emotions (i.e., have quasi-biological reactions and quasi-consciousness), not just mapping emotional data as if they had emotions.

Thinking Machines Can Be Analytical or Intuitive

The two approaches to machine intelligences result in the two types of thinking AI that we introduced in Chapter 3: the lower-level analytical AI and the higher-level intuitive AI. Analytical AI has the ability to process and synthesize large amounts of data (i.e., big data) and learn from them. Machine learning and data analytics are the major analytical AI applications. Analytical AI is "weak (or narrow) AI" that is designed to perform a narrowly defined task very well. International Business Machines Corp.'s (IBM) chess computer Deep Blue is one example. This intelligence is required for tasks that are data- and information-intensive.

The higher-level intuitive intelligence is the ability to think creatively and adjust effectively to novel situations. The AI literature considers intuitive AI as "strong (or general) AI," in that AI is designed to emulate a wide range of human cognition and learn similarly to a human child (but much faster due to its computing power and connectivity). Artificial creativity (to be discussed in Chapter 13) requires such general intelligence.

The distinction between the two types of thinking intelligence has important implications for the Feeling Economy, because being able to make decisions based on intuition and common sense is an important stepping stone to feeling AI. This has been considered by many computer scientists to be the bottleneck of AI development, which leaves to humans, at least for a while, the comparative advantage of feeling and empathy.

This distinction also implies that in the Feeling Economy less intelligent analytical AI can augment unskilled feeling labor, while the more intelligent intuitive AI can augment skilled feeling labor. Thus, the two levels of thinking AI can be applied to augment both the low-end and high-end feeling jobs and tasks.

But haven't we seen many smart machines in our daily lives that can seemingly feel? For example, the holographic Japanese AI wife, built by the company Gatebox, appears to interact, communicate, and understand her real human husband very well; conversational AI provides customer service in text, audio, and video; online feeling apps can mimic our styles of talking and comfort us emotionally. Yes, there are wide applications of seemingly feeling AI, but they are actually analytical AI with emotional data as the input and with machine learning mapping as the model. It is still mapping, but the input is emotional data.

Mechanisms for the Growth of Feeling Jobs

The distinction between the two types of thinking AI, the ways that machines mimic human intelligences, and the uniqueness of human emotions, suggest a natural way of machine–human division of labor: machines do the thinking whereas humans do the feeling.

In this scenario, human workers need to pursue one of three possible skill strategies, to retain their comparative advantage of feeling and continue having a foothold in the economy: (1) re-skilling, moving from unskilled manufacturing and thinking labor to unskilled feeling labor, (2) cross-skilling, being capable of both thinking and feeling (skilled thinking labor acquires feeling skills), and (3) up-skilling, from unskilled feeling labor to skilled feeling labor (improve feeling skills to do the feeling jobs better). Figure 4.1 illustrates the mechanisms for the growth of feeling jobs.

Unskilled Manufacturing/Thinking Labor Becomes Unskilled Service Labor

This transformation requires re-skilling. Re-skilling is to acquire a new skill set that the worker did not have before. It does not involve skill improvement; instead, it involves learning something different at the same skill level. Re-skilling is required for unskilled manufacturing labor and unskilled thinking (service) labor to survive in the Feeling Economy.

Both unskilled manufacturing workers and unskilled service workers in the thinking sector can acquire new feeling skills so that they can move to

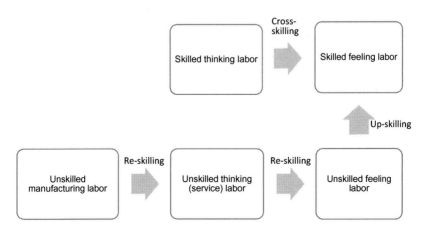

Fig. 4.1 Mechanisms for the growth of feeling employment (*Source* Authors' creation)

the "soft" feeling service sector (as alternative to the "hard" thinking service sector). Using this lens, we note that many unskilled manufacturing workers should have re-skilled in the Thinking Economy to become unskilled "hard" service labor (i.e., unskilled service labor in the thinking sectors, such as office and administrative support), as discussed in Chapter 3. So, the major move now will be for unskilled thinking service workers to re-skill to become unskilled feeling service workers. The feeling intelligence involved in such unskilled feeling service can be simple and routine, for example, a waiter in a diner needs to be able to respond and wait on customers in an emotionally appropriate manner, although those emotions may not need to be genuine or sophisticated. Frontline service employees are typical examples. One caveat for such re-skilling is that if we assume brain and heart are two separate intelligences and one who is good at one may be poor at the other, then such re-skilling may not come naturally for those thinking workers. However, in the Thinking Economy, the suppression of feeling intelligence is equally unfair to those who are naturally feeling people. It means that in the Feeling Economy our education needs to provide feeling intelligence training, just as in the Thinking Economy our education provides thinking intelligence training. We explore this in more detail in Chapter 9.

A typical example would be for a factory worker or an office secretary to become a frontline customer service agent. Answering phones and responding to customer issues based on a standard instruction manual can be relatively easily trained, as it does not involve sophisticated emotional labor. Re-skilling in this scenario can be realized faster, because from unskilled to unskilled only involves changing skills for a different sector, not improving skills for a better-paid job. Since those jobs are unskilled, re-skilling takes a shorter time than up-skilling (discussed below). However, bear in mind that mechanical AI and analytical AI can easily do this kind of job, as long as appropriate emotional data are fed to the machines. Thus, this path of job change can be expected to be easier to achieve but is less sustainable.

Unskilled Feeling Labor Improves Feeling Skills

Up-skilling is to improve feeling skills, from unskilled to skilled, so that the workers can assume higher-level feeling jobs. Up-skilling is an important path for human workers to remain competitive in the Feeling Economy. As analytical AI can be expected, as is already currently happening, to replace many unskilled feeling jobs (e.g., customer service agents), even feeling labor needs to improve their feeling skills. For example, many automobile insurance companies use in-car tracking devices (e.g., telematics devices) to track drivers' driving habits and feeling conditions (e.g., are they drowsy, drunk driving, or dangerously driving?) to decide insurance premiums, rather than having human agents to do so. We can expect to see more and more unskilled feeling jobs being done by analytical AI; thus, even feeling workers need to improve their empathetic skills to safeguard their jobs. Up-skilling takes a longer time to realize, because from unskilled to skilled takes time and is a more difficult path, typically via formal education. It means that our educational system needs to change too, to shift away from STEM education to human-skill education (more on this in Chapter 9, How Education Must Change).

Skilled Thinking Labor Acquires Feeling Skills

Cross-skilling is to acquire additional (roughly equally difficult) skills that a worker currently does not have. It expands the skills set of the worker. Cross-skilling is more applicable to those skilled thinking workers who can be trained to be empathetic as well. Cross-skilling is critical for many managerial jobs, as their jobs involve both hard and soft skills. For example, Ming-Hui Huang and Eric Wang, publishing in the journal, *Decision Science*, analogize that marketing managers are from Mars, whereas IT managers are from Venus; in many companies they don't align with each other well, costing their companies in terms of lower performance.[7] The analogy of Mars and Venus conveys the idea that one has better feeling skills and the other has better thinking skills. Both need to cross-skill so that the two sides of the brain of an organization can talk to each other for better performance. Another example is that operations managers need to be able to do statistical-based scheduling as well as communicate their scheduling decisions and suggestions to managers and subordinates. Being a purely computer and mathematical geek would not be sufficient for the Feeling Economy. In the Thinking Economy, such communication skills are not valued as much as thinking, which has created many interorganizational conflicts. In the Feeling Economy, having good soft skills is critical for the success of any project. It is for similar considerations that information management departments spin off from computer science departments to train students to be able to master management skills as well as computer skills. Unfortunately, in the Thinking Economy, the information management major often is derided as second-rate computer science, and is populated by those students who are not thinking-intelligent enough for the computer science major. In the Feeling Economy, this bias toward thinking intelligence will change.

What Characterizes the Feeling Economy?

If we say that the Thinking Economy is the present, then the Feeling Economy is the emerging future. We are not totally there yet, but we are marching toward it. In the Feeling Economy, thinking AI does the thinking, and leaves feeling jobs to humans.

Heart Women Dominate

In the Feeling Economy, we expect that females will outnumber males for higher pay feeling jobs such as health care and education. In fact, those service industries are growing much faster than manufacturing, which is stagnant or declining. This trend is exacerbated by the fact that manufacturing companies use fewer workers than they used to, because of the combination of automation and off-shoring. Jena McGregor's report in the *Washington Post* confirms this up-skilling shift. She concluded that the reason that females move up the job ladder is because their original administrative assistant jobs have been replaced by machines.[8] Based on the Labor Department data, Heather Long, also in the *Washington Post*, reports that since 2000, manufacturing workers, administrative assistants, and clerks have been the biggest job losses.[9] Those jobs (except for manufacturing workers) are dominated by women. In more academic research, Cortes, Jaimovich, and Siu, in a National Bureau of Economic Research working paper, find a general trend that they labeled as "the end of men and rise of women in the high-skilled labor market," in which there was a greater increase in demand for "female" skills (i.e., social skills, such as empathy, communication, emotion recognition, and verbal expression) in cognitive/high-wage occupations from 1980 to 2000. They consider this as due to the stronger demand for social skills over time.[10] With social skills being skills to which women are especially suited, females who up-skill themselves (when they are as college-educated as males) have an advantage in the labor market, due to their "inherent" social skills and "acquired" cognitive education. By contrast, men often need to re-skill for jobs that are traditionally female-dominated such as nursing and education.

McGregor's report provides an updated version of this prediction and explains why men take jobs in those traditionally female occupations. If those men do not take jobs in female-dominated industries, they are more likely to become unemployed, compared with their unskilled peers who are unwilling to make the move. In other words, in the Feeling Economy, females move to higher-paying jobs that are traditionally occupied by males by up-skilling (further improving their feeling skills) or cross-skilling (acquiring thinking skills by higher education), whereas males move to those jobs that are traditionally dominated by females by re-skilling (unskilled men acquire basic feeling skills) and cross-skilling (skilled thinking men acquire feeling skills). Personally, Huang hopes this comes sooner rather than later. Although Huang and Rust publish extensively together, as a male, in the prototypical Thinking Economy role of college professor, Rust is often the person who gets more of the credit. As a female, Huang complains that she is sometimes mistaken as his assistant, even if she is the first author of many of the team's papers.

There are different opinions about whether females will rise in the Feeling Economy. Some people are concerned about gender stereotyping due to machine learning. They believe that machine learning will only reinforce the existing gender stereotypes, because if the available data that machines learn from are gender-biased, then the learning outcome will be biased, leading to even worse bias (especially for reinforcement learning). For example, Joy Buolamwini from MIT's Media Lab, and Google's Timnit Gebru evaluated three commercial gender classification machine learning algorithms and found that darker females are the most misclassified. They thus urge commercial companies to develop fair facial analysis algorithms.[11] This concern does not consider that it is machines doing the thinking that reinforces the stereotypes endemic to the Thinking Economy. With machines doing more of the thinking, fewer humans need to do that thinking, and they instead move to the feeling jobs that give rise to the Feeling Economy. When machines are gender-biased, people staying in thinking jobs may be even more gender-biased, and that may speed up the migration from the Thinking to the Feeling Economy, because the Thinking Economy will shrink even faster (with more and more machines doing the thinking and fewer and fewer humans doing the thinking). The remaining Thinking Economy workers, hardcore thinking people, may be even more likely to be stereotyped, because they are likely to be the workers least capable of understanding or becoming good at "female" soft skills. By contrast, those who recognize that thinking is machine's strength will be better off moving to jobs that emphasize feeling.

Another question is whether intervention such as GWC's (Girls Who Code) effort to shorten the gender gap in tech education is in the right direction. Should we train girls to think more like boys, or should we let them be themselves (i.e., be good at social skills)? We consider that such efforts should be specific to those girls who are genuinely "thinking" types, and need an equal chance in tech, rather than generalizing to all girls, many of whom could excel at feeling-oriented tasks. In Chinese society, not just girls, but also many boys who are more social and soft skill-oriented are forced to major in STEM, resulting in personality distortion and unhappiness in work and life. For example, many students in Huang's department choose to major in information management simply because their parents wish them to do so. Many of them also end up dropping out (one became a very active blogger, one decided to take pilot training, and one couldn't find what he wants in his life) because STEM is neither what they are good at nor what they are interested in.

Soft Service Dominates

The Feeling Economy is characterized by humans returning to their human nature as feeling people, rather than training themselves to think like machines, while machines continue to excel in thinking (currently advancing from analytical to intuitive). The more advanced machines are in thinking, the more humans need to develop their soft skills for work and for life. In the Feeling Economy, thinking AI will be even more mature, and will assume many of the thinking tasks and jobs. As a result, humans will need to focus on the feeling side. Along with Maryland finance professor Max Maksimovic, we undertook empirical research to explore these changes, which we published in the AI special issue of the *California Management Review*. Our empirical evidence, based on the US government O*NET job task data and the Bureau of Labor Statistics (BLS) employment and wages data, demonstrates that, although in 2016 thinking tasks are still 14.3% more important than feeling tasks (evidence that we are still mostly in the Thinking Economy), from 2006 to 2016, feeling tasks are increasing in importance faster than thinking tasks for human jobs, evidence for the emerging Feeling Economy. During the 10 years (and we can expect a greater degree of growth in recent years with the continuing advance of AI), feeling tasks increased importance for human jobs (+5.1%), while the importance of thinking tasks remained roughly constant (+0.5%), and the importance of mechanical tasks shrank (−1.3%).

Not only are feeling tasks becoming more important, feeling-oriented sectors of the economy dominate as well. We see that the manufacturing sector dominates in the Physical Economy, and the "hard" (thinking) service sector dominates in the Thinking Economy. From manufacturing to service is a one-way ticket, as the direction of progress is from manufacturing to service, as we explained in an article in the journal, *Marketing Science*. The Feeling Economy will still be a service economy, but will be dominated by "soft service" (healthcare, management, personal care) in which feeling tasks are more important, as opposed to "hard service" (computer, engineering, legal) that dominates the Thinking Economy. Consequently, we will see that the service economy will expand on the soft side. This prediction is supported by our data in that across all major sectors, feeling tasks in general become more important over time, which is a general tendency, rather than specific to only a few industries.

To see which industries should be more important in the Feeling Economy, we calculate the relative importance of each task intelligence (mechanical, thinking, and feeling) to jobs for the 22 industries in the US government O*NET data, averaged over 2006–2016. Table 4.1 shows the top 10 industries for which feeling tasks are the most important to jobs. They include community and social service, sales and related, personal care and service, management, and food preparation and serving related. All those are high-touch services and are intensive in social interaction, emotion, and communication.

We further calculate the average employment gain or loss for the top industries shown in Table 4.1 based on data from the Occupational Employment Statistics from Bureau of Labor Statistics. Figure 4.2 shows that the growth of the feeling employment is mainly driven by the personal care and service industry (38.93%), followed by business and financial operations (24.97%) and healthcare practitioners and technical (23.90%). The growth momentum is also strong for the management (20.33%) and the food preparation and serving related (17.70%) industries (although the coronavirus pandemic may now inhibit the latter).

All the evidence indicates the emergence of the Feeling Economy: feeling tasks are becoming more important for jobs, wages for feeling tasks are rising faster, feeling industries become more important to the economy, and employment in the feeling industries is growing. These data also give us a clearer idea about what the feeling sector composed of. A more detailed list

Table 4.1 The top 10 feeling industries

1.	Community and social service
2.	Sales and related
3.	Personal care and service
4.	Management
5.	Food preparation and serving related
6.	Education, training, and library
7.	Protective service
8.	Business and financial operations
9.	Healthcare practitioners and technical
10.	Healthcare support

Source Authors' creation

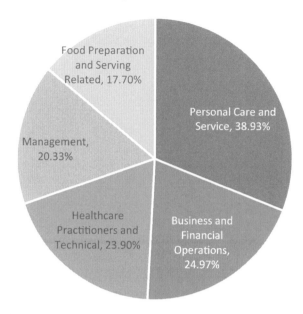

Fig. 4.2 **Fig. 4.2** Employment growth of the top 5 feeling industries (*Source* Authors' creation)

of the intelligences that correspond to particular tasks can be found in our 2019 article in the *California Management Review* AI special issue.[12]

Less Inequality?

Will we have a flatter world in the Feeling Economy eventually? The answer is: there might be a fair chance for those who are "artificially disadvantaged" in the Thinking Economy to have a better opportunity to correct this disadvantage and get their talents rewarded properly.

This potential for a more equal (inclusive) economy not only is for previously disadvantaged groups (such as females and blacks), but also for those who are artificially disadvantaged in the Thinking Economy. One of the authors presented a keynote speech at the 2019 Frontiers in Service Conference in Singapore on the topic of "The Feeling Economy," and one well-educated member of our audience appreciated very much the prediction that feeling jobs will have a fairer chance in the Feeling Economy, because his two sons are art and movie majors and he has been very worried about their future. Now he is somewhat reassured that they can do what they love, what they are good at, and still make a nice living, if the economy begins to recognize and appreciate those non-science talents and jobs. In the Feeling

Economy, many previously disadvantaged groups or individuals may have a better chance to develop their talents and to be included in the labor market. A boy who wants to become an artist does not have to suffer from majoring in science or being lectured to by parents as having no future, because in the Feeling Economy he can make a good living by soft skills.

Such a turnaround has two meanings: (1) it gives those who are "feeling-talented," but currently artificially disadvantaged in the Thinking Economy, a fairer chance in the Feeling Economy and (2) it appreciates human nature more, rather than trying to train everyone (regardless whether they are thinking or feeling people) to be a scientist or engineer. In other words, in the Feeling Economy, when feeling tasks, jobs, and sectors are emphasized more, feeling people should no longer need to force themselves into the traditional STEM education, and should no longer be disadvantaged. If they are thinking people, they need to re-skill or cross-skill themselves to at least be more intuitive, rather than simply analytical. Ultimately, even intuitive thinkers will need to gravitate more toward the feeling side.

Altogether, we expect that the growth of skilled soft service jobs will outpace the growth of unskilled soft service jobs (because mechanical feeling AI, such as chatbot customer service can easily take over such jobs), which will drive the soft service labor market toward the skilled end. We also expect that the growth of skilled soft service jobs will outpace the growth of skilled hard service jobs, which will polarize the skilled labor market into skilled thinking jobs versus skilled feeling jobs. In other words, we predict that the service labor market polarization will shift from the bimodal distribution of "unskilled versus skilled" to a new bimodal distribution of "skilled thinking vs. skilled feeling."

Those predictions, if true, will result in those who are currently artificially disadvantaged (i.e., feeling people) getting jobs (unskilled feeling jobs) and potentially getting higher-paid jobs (skilled feeling jobs) that have the potential to make the economy more equal economically, as well as richer. The implications for currently disadvantaged ethnic groups and other minorities should also be positive, as we argued earlier in the chapter.

The Economic Outcome: Relationalization

Relationalization is the major benefit (and economic output) of the Feeling Economy. We coin this term to reflect the cumulative nature of AI intelligence: once advanced to a higher level, it also has the capabilities, at least potentially, of the lower-level intelligences. Relationalization means personalization (the economic benefit of thinking intelligence) plus relationship (the economic benefit of feeling intelligence). The term conveys the idea that it is a more advanced type of personalization that requires longitudinal, unstructured emotional data as the input. Any relationship is by definition heterogeneous across individuals. Relationalization requires emotional data, which are difficult to collect, because they are personal and in context. Contextual information is often lost during data collection (see the "Lost in Translation" movie, featuring Bill Murray as a washed-up actor visiting Tokyo, for a good illustration of how losing context in translation can be hilarious).

Relationalization benefits can be realized by low-end and high-end feeling AI. The former can do unskilled feeling tasks whereas the latter (eventually) can do skilled feeling tasks.

Low-End Feeling AI

Low-end applications, such as the text-based chatbot customer service and emotional analytics, Affectiva, are analytical AI being used to analyze emotional data (e.g., voice-mining analytics for voice-based chatbots) that do unskilled feeling tasks. For example, self-service technologies are used to "automate" services that replace human labor (as discussed in the Physical Economy). The nature of the tasks is mechanical, and such feeling AI simply uses analytical AI to analyze emotional data. The current dialog systems popular in the consumer market, like Alexa, Cortana, and Siri, are another type of application that uses natural language processing to interact with customers, but in a rather mechanical manner. Most of the feeling AI falls into this category, seeking to replace many non-contextual soft service jobs.

High-End Feeling AI

High-end applications such as speech emotion recognition and simulation, such as the kinds of technology applied with the Sophia robot, are closer to true emotional machines that can experience emotion as humans in a machine way (meaning that even though they don't have physiological reactions, future neural networks can be designed to even mimic human physiological reactions). This kind of application strives to be autonomous, such that it can function independently without human intervention (e.g.,

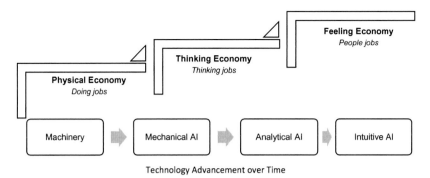

Fig. 4.3 Major technologies in the three economies (*Source* Authors' creation)

self-learn, self-act and react, self-control), in contrast to the low-end application to "automate" the operation. We don't have true emotional machines yet; thus, skilled feeling tasks are mostly performed by humans.

Together, low-end feeling AI applications apply analytical intelligence to analyze the type of emotional data that are relatively context free. It thus can deliver the economic benefit of relationalization–personalization on top of relationship.

A Summary of the Three Economies

Up to this point, we have completed the discussion of the three economies, from Physical, to Thinking, to Feeling. We illustrate the major technologies involved in the three economies in Fig. 4.3, and summarize the discussion in Table 4.2 that provides a snapshot of what they are.

How Will the Feeling Economy End?

The progress of AI is one-directional, and when feeling AI gets good enough (see Chapter 14), even feeling jobs will not be safe. We explore this more thoroughly in Chapter 15, Beyond the Feeling Economy. Meanwhile, we share a few observations.

When machines can feel like humans, or at least when they can do all the unskilled and skilled soft service jobs, we won't have the Feeling Economy. Instead, we will have a machine economy in which the human role in jobs is uncertain or even unnecessary.

Table 4.2 Summary of the three economies

	The Physical Economy	The Thinking Economy	The Feeling Economy
Definition	Employment and wages are more attributable to mechanical/physical tasks	Employment and wages are more attributable to analytical/thinking tasks	Employment and wages are more attributable to empathetic/feeling tasks
Characteristics	• Muscle men dominate • Manufacturing dominates • More opportunity for less-skilled workers	• Brain people dominate • Service dominates • Inequality of wealth	• Heart women dominate • Soft service dominates • Less inequality?
Driving technology	Machinery (manufacturing technology) • Machines that provide tools to enable production of all manufactured goods	Mechanical AI (or IT): • IT: Systems of computers store and process data and update from it • Mechanical AI: machines learns and adapts minimally	Thinking AI • Analytical AI: Machines learn and adapt based on data (i.e., mapping) • Intuitive AI: Machines learn and adapt based on knowledge (i.e., reasoning)
Human skill	Physical strength (unskilled)	Rational thinking (hard skills)	Empathy and feeling (soft skills)
Mechanism	• Machinery de-skills jobs, allowing unskilled labor to participate in manufacturing	• Mechanical AI replaces unskilled manufacturing labor and augments skilled service labor	• Thinking AI replaces unskilled and skilled thinking labor and augments feeling labor

	The Physical Economy	The Thinking Economy	The Feeling Economy
Employment	The physical employment expands due to: • De-skilling: Machinery de-skills manufacturing jobs • Re-skilling: Unskilled agriculture labor becomes unskilled manufacturing labor	The thinking employment expands due to: • Re-skilling: Unskilled manufacturing labor becomes unskilled service labor • Up-skilling: Unskilled service labor becomes skilled thinking (service) labor	The feeling employment expands due to: • Re-skilling: Unskilled manufacturing labor and unskilled thinking (service) labor becomes unskilled feeling (service) labor • Up-skilling: Unskilled feeling labor improves their feeling intelligence to become skilled feeling labor • Cross-skilling: Skilled thinking labor acquires feeling skills
Wages	Most unskilled manufacturing workers are employed with relatively low average wages.	High wages to skilled thinking workers, physical workers and feeling workers get lower wages	High wages to skilled feeling workers, physical workers and thinking workers get lower wages
Major industry	Manufacturing (i.e., the Physical Economy)	Hard service (i.e., the Thinking Economy)	Soft service (i.e., the Feeling Economy)
Major economic benefit	Standardization	Personalization	Relationalization

Source Authors' creation

What will happen to humans if machines can feel? People have different views on this. The optimistic view considers that when machines become smarter than humans in all levels of intelligence, machines will do all the work and humans will have all the fun. It is an ideal form of work-life arrangement, with machines being producers and with humans being consumers. In this happy scenario, human working hours shrink to zero and they can use all the hours on lives. In 2017, Ray Kurzweil, futurist and Google's Director of Engineering, said that in the technological singularity, "We're going to get more neocortex, we're going to be funnier, we're going to be better at music. We're going to be sexier. We're really going to exemplify all the things that we value in humans to a greater degree."[13] It implies that the current economic arrangement will need to be restructured, because income/salary/money does not hinge on work, and thus how humans are going to pay for their consumption is an issue. Are we to assume that consumption will be all free because they are produced by machines?

The pessimistic view considers that when machines outsmart humans, they won't be so stupid as to do all the work and let humans have all the fun. It is more likely to be the other way around, with humans doing all the work and machines enjoy their "machine" lives. Or, since humans are not even good for work (because machines are better for all mechanical, thinking, and feeling tasks), they are no longer needed in the world. In this scenario, it will be a time in which only machines survive in the world (survival of the fittest). We explore these issues in greater detail in Chapter 15.

Conclusions

The Feeling Economy is the natural next step resulting from the continuing development of AI. We are so immersed in the Thinking Economy today that it is often difficult to imagine a world in which human thinking intelligence is less valued. Thinking intelligence, in general, will be more important than ever, but it will increasingly be done by machines. This leaves feeling intelligence as the remaining safe haven, for a few decades, for human workers.

Notes

1. Neuroscience (2019), *Nature*, https://www.nature.com/subjects/neuroscience.
2. Morgan, C. Lloyd (1903), *An Introduction to Comparative Psychology*, 2nd ed. London: Walter Scott.

3. Pavlov, Ivan (1960), *Conditional Reflexes*, New York: Dover Publications.
4. Skinner, B. F. (1938), *The Behavior of Organisms: An Experimental Analysis*, Oxford: Appleton-Century.
5. Schoenick, Carissa, Peter Clark, Oyvind Tafjord, Peter Turney, and Oren Etzioni (2017), "Moving Beyond the Turing Test with the Allen AI Science," *Communications of the ACM*, 60 (9), 60–64.
6. Darwiche, Andan (2018), "Human-Level Intelligence or Animal-Like Abilities?" *Communications of the ACM*, 61 (10), 56–67.
7. Huang, Ming-Hui, and Eric T. G. Wang (2013), "Marketing Is from Mars, IT Is from Venus: Aligning the Worldviews for Firm Performance," *Decision Sciences*, 44 (1), 87–125.
8. McGregor, Jena (2020), "The Shock of Unemployment May Push Men into Jobs Traditionally Held by Women, Study Shows," *The Washington Post*, January 15, https://www.washingtonpost.com/business/2020/01/15/shock-unemploym ent-may-push-men-into-jobs-traditionally-held-by-women-study-shows/.
9. Long, Heather (2019), "Administrative Assistant Jobs Helped Propel Many Women into the Middle Class. Now They're Disappearing," *The Washington Post*, December 5, https://www.washingtonpost.com/business/economy/admini strative-assistant-jobs-helped-propel-many-women-into-the-middle-class-now- theyre-disappearing.
10. Cortes, Guido Matias, Nir Jaimovich, and Henry E. Siu (2018), "The 'End of Men' and Rise of Women in the High-Skilled Labor Market," NBER Working Paper 24274.
11. Buolamwini, Joy, and Timnit Gebru (2018), "Gender Shades: Intersectional Accuracy Disparities in Commercial Gender Classification," Proceedings of the 1st Conference on Fairness, Accountability and Transparency, *Proceedings of Machine Learning Research (PMLR)*, 81, 77–91.
12. Huang, Ming-Hui, Roland T. Rust, and Vojislav Maksimovic (2019), "The Feeling Economy: Managing in the Next Generation of AI," *California Management Review*, 64 (4), 43–65.
13. Youngdahl, William E., and B. Tom Hunsaker (2018), "SingularityNET: Blockhain-Driven AI Marketplace and Quest for AGI," Thunderbird School of Global Management Case.

5

The Age of Emoji

As the Feeling Economy emerges, and AI assumes more thinking tasks, people are increasingly focusing on emotion. One notable way this trend is manifested is the increasing use of emoticons (typographical tricks that resemble pictures) and emoji (plug-in graphics that are actual pictures). Such emotional communication has become ubiquitous on social media and the Internet. Those technologies have deconstructed time, physical distance, and emotional distance, making emotional connection possible even when people are far apart, and even when their communication is separated in time. This greater access to emotional communication makes emotional intelligence more important than ever. We even see the emotionalization of the creative arts, such as music, as AI becomes more involved in artistic production.

The Rise of Emoji

Emoticons (emotion icons) first appeared in the Internet world, as the cold, computerized environment pushed users to work harder to express themselves emotionally. For example, a person who wished to express happiness might use a smiley face emoticon:

:-)

They were first invented by Carnegie Mellon computer scientist Scott Fahlman in 1982.[1]

Not coincidentally, Fahlman is also thought to have received the first PhD specifically on the topic of artificial intelligence, from MIT in 1977.[2]

© The Author(s) 2021
R. T. Rust and M.-H. Huang, *The Feeling Economy*,
https://doi.org/10.1007/978-3-030-52977-2_5

Fig. 5.1 Emoji (*Source* https://publicdomainvectors.org/en/tag/emoji)

The connection between the development of AI and the increased need for emotional expression could not be clearer.

From the first smiley face (and frowny face) proposed by Professor Fahlman, emoticons quickly expanded to a wide range of emotional expression,[3] ranging from crying:

:'-(

to surprise:

:O

to a wink:

;-)

People realized that not all of these emoticons were easy to read and understand, which eventually led to the invention of emoji in Japan, appearing on Japanese mobile phones in 1997. They are now available on many mobile phone systems, email software, and word processing packages worldwide. Most emoji are copyrighted, but many also appear in the public domain, including the following[4] (Fig. 5.1):

Emoji have become so important that an emoji was named "word of the year" by Oxford Dictionaries in 2015.[5] The increasing importance of emoji is a direct result of AI's increasing capability, combined with modern social media.

Physical and Emotional Distance

With the smartphone (AI in a pocket) taking over more of the thinking tasks, human communication turns more toward emotion, expressed at a distance. Direct personal contact is reduced, and contact at a distance is facilitated. Constant contact with minimum intrusiveness demands technologies such as email, and especially texting. Unlike sound (or multimedia) conversations, which involve high bandwidth and convey extensive emotional nuance, the print environment of email and text is relatively emotionally impoverished.

It is in this environment that emotional signs such as emoticons and emoji become particularly needed. In other words, maintaining a close emotional distance becomes even more of a priority when physical distance is a barrier, and bandwidth is limited. As AI works harder on the thinking side, humans have to work harder emotionally.

Social Media and Personal Connections

The Feeling Economy emphasizes emotion and empathy. It is hardly a coincidence that the proliferation of emoticons and emoji has occurred during the time of the emerging Feeling Economy. People everywhere are seeking to express emotion more quickly and efficiently. Consumers who can no longer multiply two numbers together can nevertheless draw upon an extensive menu of possible emotional symbols to communicate. The former thinking machines (people) are now increasingly emotional and interpersonal beings.

Exemplifying this shift is the expansion of social media. Platforms such as Facebook and Instagram connect people emotionally. Maybe not all of the "friends" on Facebook are real friends, but it is easier than ever to communicate with others and to follow what they do. The ability to communicate skillfully on social media is one of today's most essential skills, and increasingly the most important key to commercial success. It is also not an accident that platforms such as Facebook, Twitter, Instagram, and even smartphone texting have supplanted email as the medium of choice when communicating emotional messages. These messages are often visual (e.g., Instagram) as much or more than textual, and even text is now embellished with emoji or emoticons.

Emotional Intelligence

Daniel Goleman's 1995 book, *Emotional Intelligence*,[6] made the case that IQ is not enough, and that emotional intelligence (EQ) is equally or more important. Since publication, the message of that book has become increasingly timely, as AI has forced HI to focus on feeling intelligence to an unprecedented degree. Emotional intelligence has always been important, but it has never been as important as it is today.

Emotional intelligence is inherently social. It involves perceiving and understanding other people's emotions, and then responding to them in an emotionally appropriate way. The more social a relationship, the more

emotional intelligence is key. For example, emotional intelligence is abso-
lutely critical in a marriage. It is also of vital importance in relationships
with customers, and in relationships with coworkers. Although it is possible
to succeed to a degree in business and in life with minimal emotional
intelligence (think the chess player Bobby Fischer, or "geek" computer
programmers), such cases typically involve people with exceptional thinking
intelligence. As AI gradually attains those same capabilities (e.g., IBM's Deep
Blue defeating world chess champion Gary Kasparov), antisocial brainy types
decline in value. The emotional, empathetic, and interpersonal skills, harder
for AI to do, become the human skills that are in the greatest demand.

Emotion in Music

One might expect the creative arts to be immune to the AI invasion, since
creativity is often thought to be an inherently human quality. This turns
out not to be the case. Let us consider the example of music. AI got
a start in music in the early twentieth century, when some avant garde
classical composers such as Arnold Schoenberg and John Cage inserted
random and/or computational elements into their composition. Even George
Gershwin, a writer of popular songs who also had one foot in the classical
world, used randomized elements to help in his composition. Computa-
tionally based approaches really took off, though, with the proliferation of
computerization.

As computers became faster and cheaper, they played a bigger role in the
music world. Synthesizers (think of as AI for making music), first made
inroads in popular music in the 1960s, using innovative instruments such as
the Moog synthesizer, which was used by such popular bands as the Monkees,
the Doors, Pink Floyd, and the Beatles. Over time, the increasing use of
synthesized music began to make music seem cold and impersonal. Bands
such as Kraftwerk and Tangerine Dream built sound structures that seemed
to include humans only as an afterthought.

The reaction to AI's invasion of music took two forms. One was an
outright rejection of AI, and even of human playing that sounded mechanical. This was manifested in the punk revolution of the late 1970s, led by
bands such as the Ramones and the Sex Pistols, which emphasized intense,
almost cartoonish, levels of emotion. This led to the development of "emo"
music, an extension of punk music that greatly exaggerated the emotional
element. It also led to "grunge" music in the 1990s, such as Nirvana, which
saw itself as a continuation of the punk tradition. Fighting AI was ultimately a

losing battle, and it is perhaps not a surprise that many of the musicians who raged the hardest against the AI revolution (e.g., Kurt Cobain, Sid Vicious, Chris Cornell, Chester Bennington) are prematurely dead.[7]

The second kind of reaction to the AI music invasion was to not reject AI, but to collaborate with it. David Bowie was an early pioneer of this. In albums made with early synthesizer pioneer Brian Eno, Bowie used a hyper-emotional vocal style to counterbalance the coldness of the instrumentation. The British synthesizer band, Ultravox, was another early proponent of this direction. Today, popular music (think Taylor Swift) is dominated by AI-driven synthesizer riffs and rhythm tracks, with highly emotional vocals over the top. This has created some unlikely collaborations, such as folk singer Ellie Goulding teaming up with electronica artist Calvin Harris. Most dance/electronica recordings, for example, make use of emotional vocals to counteract the coldness of the AI-driven musical structure. As a general rule, the more AI/synthesizer-oriented the backing music, the more emotional the vocals need to be. This is especially the case in dance/electronica recordings.

Should We Use Emoticons in Serving Customers?

With business becoming more feeling-oriented, it would seem to make sense for business people to begin to use more emoticons when interacting with customers. One recent academic article suggests some caveats, however. Hong Kong researchers Li, Chan, and Kim show that emoticons lead customers to believe the service provider is warmer but less competent.[8] Furthermore, there are two kinds of customers who respond differently to emoticons. "Communal-oriented" customers are positively affected by emoticon use, whereas "exchange-oriented" customers are negatively affected. Translating these terms to our viewpoint, we see communal-oriented customers as being more relationship-oriented and more feeling-oriented, while exchange-oriented customers are more transactional and rational. Given the long-term trend in the economy toward relationships and feeling, the findings from their research suggest that the use of emoticons by businesses should increase over time.

Conclusions

The more an AI/HI collaboration is controlled by AI, the more emotional HI needs to be. We see this in communication on the smartphone, in which emoticons, and then emoji, have become increasingly used. As social media have made communication at a distance (and often time-shifted) indispensable, emotion must be turned up to counteract the lack of bandwidth in the communication. This has encouraged the growing use of visuals and multimedia, and platforms such as Instagram, to increase the emotional content in messages. Correspondingly, the importance of emotional intelligence has increased, as the skills of emotionally challenged thinking workers have been taken over by AI. Even in the creative arts, the AI invasion has forced humans to become more emotional, as part of the creation that is uniquely human has shrunk. Even businesses will likely find that they can relate to the modern, feeling-oriented consumer by using emoticons. The Feeling Economy is an age of emoji—an era in which emotion is prized, and humans cry out to be recognized for their humanness.

Notes

1. Bignell, Paul (2012), "Happy 30th Birthday, Emoticon!:-)" *Independent* (September 9), accessed August 14, 2019.
2. Fahlman, Scott (2019), "Who Was the First Person to Get a PhD Degree Specifically in 'Artificial Intelligence,' *Quora* (March 5, 2019), accessed August 14, 2019.
3. *Wikipedia* (2019), "List of Emoticons," accessed August 14, 2019.
4. "Happy Green Positive Face Emoticon Vector Illustration," publicdomainvectors.org, accessed August 14, 2019.
5. Oxford Dictionaries (2015), "English Word of the Year," Oxford University Press.
6. Goleman, Daniel (1995), *Emotional Intelligence*, New York: Bantam Books.
7. Kornhaber, Spencer (2018), "The Sound of Rage and Sadness," *The Atlantic*, 322 (1), 30–32.
8. Li, Xueni (Shirley), Kimmy Wa Chan and Sara Kim (2019), "Service with Emoticons: How Customers Interpret Employee Use of Emoticons in Online Service Encounters," *Journal of Consumer Research*, 45 (5), 973–987.

6

Jobs That Feel

In Chapter 1, we mentioned two examples of jobs that have changed in the last few years due to AI. We mentioned how such jobs as financial analyst are becoming less technical, due to AI taking over much of the thinking aspects. Financial analysts are instead left to focus on relationships with clients. Similarly, customer service representatives have fewer routine responsibilities, because those have largely been taken over by chatbots. The result is that customer service representatives have been "upgraded," spending more of their time on nonroutine client issues and deeper customer interactions. We will see that collaborating with AI inevitably changes the nature of human jobs, typically resulting in upgraded job definitions and higher levels of responsibility. To keep up with these changes, companies must not only upgrade existing jobs, but also should seek to create new feeling-oriented jobs. Government data show us where the feeling jobs are, and which jobs are growing the fastest. To stay ahead of the game, workers also need to reinvent themselves to be a better fit for the kinds of jobs that will dominate the Feeling Economy.

How Collaborating with AI Changes the Job

Let us consider the job of a taxi driver. At first glance, this appears to be a blue-collar, low-skilled job. It is mostly physical, but also involves thinking intelligence (e.g., figuring out the right route, responding to road conditions) and feeling intelligence (e.g., interacting with passengers). AI has already made large inroads on this job, and promises even more disruption in the

© The Author(s) 2021
R. T. Rust and M.-H. Huang, *The Feeling Economy*,
https://doi.org/10.1007/978-3-030-52977-2_6

future. Consider the problem of finding the right route. AI, in the form of GPS navigation software such as Waze, has already assumed much of the job of finding out where to go. This has largely freed human labor from knowing the area. In London, by contrast, the taxi drivers must take an exam called "the knowledge," to prove that they know how to find just about anything. Navigation software makes that skill obsolete. Ride sharing companies, such as Uber and Lyft, have been able to disrupt the taxi industry as a result, using part-time drivers who use AI for much of the thinking task. Thus, Uber, for example, pays much more attention to its drivers' customer satisfaction scores (reflecting the drivers' people skills) than it does to the drivers' route knowledge. As AI improves its thinking intelligence, the disruption to the taxi industry will be even larger. Sufficient analytical and intuitive intelligence will make possible self-driving taxis that replace drivers altogether. Meanwhile, however, the taxi driver job requires less thinking intelligence, and feeling intelligence and people skills assume more importance.

Another job that is currently being transformed is that of baseball umpire. One of the most important tasks for an umpire is deciding balls and strikes. Umpires are human, which means they are quite capable of missing calls, which drives the players crazy. As a result, the sport of baseball has been seeking ways to use AI more and increase the accuracy of these calls. The first step was to use AI-fueled pitch tracking to evaluate every pitch. The human umpires are then graded according to how accurately they call balls and strikes. In 2019, a professional baseball league took the next step, creating an elaborate system in which AI and HI collaborate to evaluate each pitch. AI (the pitch tracker) decides whether a pitch is a ball or strike. A human in the press box then relays that information to the umpire, who is wearing an earplug. The umpire has the right to overrule the AI decision on the pitch, in case something is obviously wrong. Early feedback regarding the system is positive, with players, umpires, and fans seeing very little disruption and even higher confidence in the correctness of the calls. The umpire still has the people-facing, feeling role, but AI has assumed much of the thinking role, at least for balls and strikes. Even the top level of baseball competition, the major leagues in the United States, are moving very quickly to AI in calling balls and strikes, and the expectation is that it will be widely applied at the highest levels by 2021.

Upgrading Existing Jobs

If we evaluate the levels of intelligence as being from physical to thinking to feeling, in the order of difficulty for AI to emulate, then as AI assumes more tasks at the lower levels of intelligence, HI must be upgraded to focus on the higher levels of intelligence. This typically leaves the human worker with more responsibility and a more interesting job, compared to before, as AI assumes more of the physical and mechanical tasks, and increasingly the thinking tasks as well.

Let us consider, for example, the job of an immigration officer at an international airport. Traditionally there has been a very long line of people, and the immigration officer checks the passport (and visa, when necessary) of every arriving international passenger. This job involves a considerable amount of mindless routine, and many of the thinking tasks required are easily automated. Many airports around the world have installed automatic scanning technologies that can read a passport, read fingerprints, or even recognize faces. The result of this technology is that fewer immigration officers are typically required, and many of those who remain have an upgraded job that focuses more on difficult cases and nonroutine interactions with arriving passengers.

Even professional services are not immune from these developments. As an example, AI has proved to be even more accurate than humans in evaluating some key medical test results, such as electrocardiograms. IBM's Watson system is one example of a commercially available AI technology in the medical field. Interestingly, the reception of Watson has been lukewarm. Apparently the people-oriented feeling skills are not its strength. The human doctors, who have better feeling skills, seem to be valued more, even when they are less accurate. This indicates the direction that professional service needs to go. The human service provider (the doctor) needs to collaborate more effectively with AI. Upgrading the job in this case means that the doctor must focus on the feeling skills that help the doctor interact successfully with patients. A doctor with outstanding feeling intelligence may be able to make the patient comfortable with the use of AI. Outstanding feeling intelligence may also help the doctor absorb the blow to his/her ego caused by delegating some of the thinking tasks to AI!

Another example is fraud detection in banking or taxation. This used to be done by humans randomly checking (auditing), and using judgment to decide whether there was a problem. Today, the initial screen of records is done by AI. Because of the large amounts of data available for training, neural network (deep learning) methods can be trained to be very accurate in identifying fraudulent activity. This leaves the humans in fraud detection to focus on a smaller number of likely problem cases. The result is that fewer such people are needed, but those that are needed must have a higher level of skill, much of which involves the feeling intelligence and people skills necessary to communicate effectively with people when following up on the problem.

Research in marketing investigates the effect of empathy on designer performance. The academic findings, supported by managerial experience, show that designers who are more empathetic can create better and more innovative products, especially as customers become more feeling-oriented.[1]

Creating New Feeling Jobs

When the Physical Economy gave way to the Thinking Economy, many Physical Economy jobs were lost, and many physical workers were displaced. That was not the end of the story, though, as the Thinking Economy began to generate many new jobs of its own. Replacing many coal mining, farming, and factory jobs were new jobs in things like coding, data science, and working in the rapidly expanding service economy. These new jobs required different skills and training, but they presented a great opportunity to those willing to move into the newer parts of the economy. As the Thinking Economy gives way to the Feeling Economy, we expect a similar dynamic to unfold. Although many Thinking Economy jobs will be lost, there are also likely to be many new opportunities in the Feeling Economy. Such jobs may require different training than Thinking Economy jobs did.

These new Feeling Economy jobs won't all involve direct personal relationships with customers. Some of those jobs will be about using AI to help customers relate to each other better. Many of these new jobs are entrepreneurial opportunities. For example, in the coronavirus crisis of 2020, one opportunistic entrepreneur created the Quarantine Together dating app, to help people stranded at home pair up with others.[2] AI does the thinking work of the site, but it took an empathetic inventor to perceive the opportunity.

Growth Jobs for the Feeling Economy

Where are the best growth job opportunities for the Feeling Economy? CNBC mined US government data from the Bureau of Labor Statistics to find the 27 jobs that pay more than $100,000 per year, and are expected to grow more than 10% between 2016 and 2026.[3] The list is enlightening, because it makes it quite clear that the Feeling Economy jobs dominate. Although six of the 27 jobs are classic Thinking Economy jobs (petroleum engineers, scientists, computer and information systems workers, software developers and actuaries, physicists and astronomers), the other 21 represent the fast-growing Feeling Economy, in that they emphasize direct human contact, either as a direct service provider or a manager. Of those, 15 are in the medical and health care fields. The other six jobs are all managerial.

Taking a broader look at the same data, if we list the top 10 industries in terms of the importance of feeling tasks, we see a very similar pattern.[4] Of the 10 industries, nine are service jobs of various types (e.g., sales, personal care, medical, etc.), and management also appears on the list. The only clearly Thinking Economy industry on the list is business and financial operations, which may be considered primarily analytical. Even there, the Feeling Economy is encroaching, as we can see from the financial analyst example that we discussed earlier, in which the importance of feeling tasks is increasing.

Career Strategies for the Feeling Economy

The safest career strategy is always to be in a growth job in a growth industry. We have seen from the previous sections that the fastest growing industries focus on either healthcare or management, and the fastest growing attractive jobs are almost all people-facing jobs. We also know that the service sector of every developed economy has been growing steadily for more than 100 years, as the goods sector stagnates.[5] These facts make clear the best career strategy for the Feeling Economy. A job seeker should focus on the service sector—either health care or other services—and choose a people-facing job.

Interestingly, these people-focused, service-oriented jobs have traditionally hired a disproportionate number of women. We explore the implications for women in Chapter 7. But even for men, moving into "womens' work" may be the right thing to do. University of Texas sociologist Christine Williams has researched this topic,[6] and found that when men receive the "shock" of losing their traditionally male job (e.g., factory work), 19% of the time they end up in traditionally female jobs. Moving forward, men may need to embrace the traditionally female jobs to an unprecedented extent.

That is all fine for someone who is just starting out, but what about someone who is already entrenched in a Thinking Economy job, or who lacks the people skills to be successful in a typical Feeling Economy job. For the person who is in a typical Thinking Economy job (e.g., a coder or data scientist) the successful path is fairly clear. Observing that AI is likely to assume an increasing number of the technical tasks, the thinking worker should seek to move into a supervisory position. Such managerial positions will be slow to be taken over by AI. Such a manager must be knowledgeable about the technical side as well as the people side, which means the best managerial candidates are likely to come from the pool of technical workers. The thinking worker should seek opportunities to lead teams, with the end goal of assuming a higher position in management.

For the thinking worker who lacks strong people skills, the key is developing those skills. As we will see in Chapter 9, "executive education" focusing on technical workers who want to move into management is likely to be an important growth area in management education. The thinking worker should make her supervisors know that she is interested in the managerial track, and seize any opportunity to pursue personal development with respect to leadership skills and dealing with people.

Conclusions

Physical work did not go away when the Thinking Economy emerged—it was just done more often by machine. Similarly, thinking work will not go away as the Feeling Economy emerges—however, it will increasingly be done by AI. The human jobs that remain will gravitate to people-oriented work such as service and management. Humans and AI will collaborate as teams, with AI being the technical expert and HI being the people expert. Existing jobs will be "upgraded" to focus on the "higher" feeling intelligence. Even as fewer thinking workers are required, there will be demand for more feeling workers, who can focus on human relationships. The fastest growing jobs are almost all in the emerging Feeling Economy. To be successful in this coming era of AI, workers should welcome the Feeling Economy and its emphasis on people skills. They should seek either a direct service job or a managerial job, neither of which is likely to be in jeopardy in the medium term.

Notes

1. Steimer, Sarah (2019), "But How Does That Make You *Feel?*" *Marketing News*, September, 44–51.
2. *Quarantine Together* (2020), accessed at https://www.quarantinetogether.com/ on April 7, 2020.

3. CNBC (2018), "The 27 Fastest-Growing Jobs That Pay More Than $100,000 Per Year," https://www.msn.com/en-us/money/careersandeducation/the-27-fastest-growing-jobs-that-pay-more-than-dollar100000-a-year/ar-BBRdER5, accessed August 21, 2019.
4. Huang, Ming-Hui, Roland T. Rust, and Vojislav Maksimovic (2019), "The Feeling Economy: Managing in the Next Generation of Artificial Intelligence," *California Management Review*, 61 (4), 43–65.
5. Rust, Roland T., and Ming-Hui Huang (2014), "The Service Revolution and the Transformation of Marketing Science," *Marketing Science*, 33 (2), 206–221.
6. McGregor, Jena (2020), "Shock of Job Loss May Push Men into Work Traditionally Held by Women," *Washington Post*, January 21, A11.

7

The Era of Women

When we consider the beneficiaries of AI, we often visualize robots such as the Terminator, raising macho havoc on society. But as the Feeling Economy emerges from the development of AI, one group of people seems uniquely positioned to benefit. We may be beginning to experience the era of women.

The history of automation and AI turns out to involve a steady decline in the status and importance of men, along with a steady increase in the status and importance of women. The Physical Economy was dominated by men, with their larger size and bigger muscles. As physical tasks were automated, the Thinking Economy emerged, which was a much more favorable environment for women. Throughout the Thinking Economy, signs of women's progress have been accelerating, reflected by such things as women's right to vote,[1] a proposed Equal Rights Amendment and Title IX in the United States, and increasing participation by women in the military, sports, business, academia, and politics. This progress is sure to accelerate further, as women assume unprecedented status and importance in the Feeling Economy.

The Physical Economy and the Era of Men

In the Physical Economy, physical strength was prized, and men, who on average are bigger and stronger than women, seized a dominant position. Occupations like farming, mining, construction, factory work, and the military required physical strength, putting men at an advantage, which was reflected broadly in men's higher status. Men also assumed most of the most

© The Author(s) 2021
R. T. Rust and M.-H. Huang, *The Feeling Economy*,
https://doi.org/10.1007/978-3-030-52977-2_7

powerful positions in society. For example, prior to 1972 all Fortune 500 CEOs were men, and prior to 1984 all candidates for US President or Vice President were men. These historical advantages have led to a sort of male entitlement, in which some conservative elements in society would like to "turn back the clock" to reestablish male dominance. For example, President Trump's former nominee for the Federal Reserve, Stephen Moore, was quoted as saying, "The problem has actually been the steady decline in male earnings."[2] Notably, Moore focused on male earnings even though female earnings show a continuing (albeit declining) pay gap.[3]

The Thinking Economy and the Rise of Women

As the Thinking Economy supplanted the Physical Economy, women gained the ability to compete with men on a more equal basis. This has led to many advances in the position of women in society. As the Thinking Economy has emerged, women's progress has been profound, and has affected virtually all corners of the society.

Between 1893 and 1930, as automation was assuming greater importance in manufacturing, women's suffrage was granted in almost all of Western Europe, the United States, New Zealand (first, in 1893), and Australia. By comparison the nations that had not installed women's suffrage by 1975 were a who's who of economic backwaters, including Portugal, Namibia, Samoa, Kazakhstan, and Moldova, plus Mideast oil countries such as Kuwait, the UAE, and Saudi Arabia. (Ironically, women's rights laggard Saudi Arabia recently became the first country to name an AI citizen, the "female" robot Sophia.)

The push for greater rights for women does not end with suffrage. For example, in the United States there has been proposed an Equal Rights Amendment that would guarantee equal rights to all on the basis of gender. Along similar lines, the United States in 1972 passed legislation (known as Title IX) that protects women's rights (and effectively demands equivalent funding) in education.

Even in formerly Physical Economy jobs such as the military, women have made significant advances. This should not be surprising, given that the physical tasks of the military have to a great extent been assumed by mechanization, assisted by AI-enabled computerization. With AI controlling much of the mechanical work, humans are left to handle the thinking and interpersonal tasks—tasks for which women are just as suited as men. Thus, although some military units, such as US Special Forces, remain mostly off-limits for women, due to their exceptional physical demands, for most military jobs, including combat, women are now treated as men's equals.

The shift from Physical Intelligence, to Thinking Intelligence, to Feeling Intelligence, has been a shift that has favored women, and that shift has been recognized by the population. For example, in 1946, before the Thinking Economy reached its peak, only 35% of Americans viewed women as being as intelligent as men. By 2018, 86% of Americans viewed the genders as equally intelligent, and most of those who viewed the two genders differently thought that women were more intelligent.[4]

Does AI Always Boost Women?

As the previous sections explain, the shift to the Feeling Economy should be very favorable for women, because the Feeling Economy skills (empathy, etc.) are those in which women have an advantage, on average. Does this mean that AI is always a positive force for women's inequality? It turns out that this is not always the case.

Due in great part to the inertia caused by the male-dominated past in the Thinking Economy, and especially the Physical Economy, women have frequently been discriminated against in the past, and still are, in many countries around the world. In the economics literature, such discrimination is known as "taste for discrimination," and is not necessarily caused by rational factors.[5] This kind of discrimination is bigotry, and it is endemic in human history.

With the advent of AI, it was hoped that discrimination would mostly end, because AI can evaluate factors in an objective and rational manner. However, it has been shown that even an impartial algorithm can discriminate against groups such as women,[6] even if the protected group (e.g., women, racial minorities, religious minorities, etc.) is not explicitly used by the algorithm.[7] For example, women might be discriminated against for bank loans or credit limits, if some variables that correlate with gender (e.g., income) are less favorable.[8]

Gender Differences in Brain Physiology

Although women have mostly the same mental capabilities as men, there are some statistically significant differences between the sexes.[9] For example, men's brains tend to be more laterally differentiated, corresponding to greater spatial ability. Men, on average, tend to have more ability to know how an object will appear, if rotated, and what will happen to an object, if fired through the air. These specific male skills are quite related to the skills necessary in the Physical Economy (e.g., spear throwing), and also give men an edge with respect to spatially involved activities such as mathematics and chess.

Gender differences in the brain are controversial to discuss, because such differences have been used in the past to discriminate against less privileged groups. For example, Nobel Prize winner William Shockley may as well have been William "Shocking" when he claimed that other races were inferior to the Europeans, and advocated eugenics—something the Nazis also advocated. Nevertheless, it is widely accepted today that the genders do differ, on average, in how the brain is constructed.

Surprisingly, there has been relatively little research comparing genders, due to the controversial nature of the topic, and misguided attempts to "control" for the erratic influence of hormones, which some studies have shown have more variance in women.[10] Perhaps the most influential academic research on gender differences was conducted by a team of researchers at the University of Pennsylvania. That research, which was published in 2014 in the *Proceedings of the National Academy of Sciences*, found that men and women, on average, had different kinds of inter-brain connections. Ironically, AI, in the form of deep learning neural nets, has even been used to study brain differences between the genders, again concluding that they exist.

The upshot is that men (on average) should be better at action-oriented, spatial thinking, while women should be better at interpersonal and communal thinking. All researchers in this research area emphasize that intra-group variation swamps the intergroup variation, which means that there can be women who are terrific at spatial skills (e.g., soccer star Megan Rapinoe) and men who can be very empathetic (e.g., politician Joe Biden).

It can be shown mathematically that two populations that differ a small amount, on average, can nevertheless result in a predominance of the superior group when examining the top performers. Thus, we see that of the 60 winners of the Fields Medal (for the top mathematician under 40), only one woman, Maryam Mirzakhani, has won. A similar situation is seen in chess, where the 2020 FIDE list of the top chess players in the world shows the top woman, Yifan Hou of China, is only ranked #75. The first author (Rust) was also a tournament chess player, who played for his college chess teams as an undergraduate and graduate student, but he freely admits that Ms. Hou could crush him across the chessboard nearly every time (giving Rust the questionable benefit of the doubt that she would not beat him *every* time).

Huang, for example, is a capable time-series econometrician, who often takes on the statistical modeling in papers that she writes. In other words, the top women in mathematics and chess are still very, very good. Nevertheless, they are not quite as good, on average, as men, which has given men an advantage in mathematical/spatial aspects of the Thinking Economy.

This is not to ignore that there are also cultural factors in play. For example, in some countries, girls are not permitted to go to school. In such a case, they can hardly become mathematicians! Even in more developed countries, there can be subtle discouragement of women who attempt to excel at "male" pursuits. These cultural factors can exacerbate gender differences.

Things all reverse in the Feeling Economy. All of those special mathematical/spatial abilities may not be as valuable once AI can do them better than humans. AI can already defeat the top human chess players and go players (go is considered an even more complex game than chess). As those skills are assumed by AI, what is left for people is feeling, and that is where women excel.[11] Women have evolved to take care of children and nurture families. We also acknowledge that many women may be forced into such a role, due to political and cultural pressures, no matter whether they have other interests and aptitudes.

Nevertheless, the evolutionary advantage from women's traditional child-rearing role means that their less laterally specific brains can do a better job, on average, of holistic reasoning and reading of emotions. Although there is debate as to whether nature or nurture is to blame for this, a very large-scale Cambridge study of more than 600,000 people, using the Empathizing-Systemizing theory of sex differences, verified that women are more empathetic and men are more systematic. That study notes that the STEM tasks that are valued in the Thinking Economy tend to be male strengths, on average. We note that because women are more empathetic, their contributions are likely to be much more valued in the Feeling Economy, as the kind of thinking men are best at is deemphasized (taken over by AI).

The Feeling Economy—Women on Top

The preceding arguments suggest that as the economy advances, women should assume more power and influence. That was true as the economy transitioned from the Physical Economy to the Thinking Economy, and it should be even truer as the economy transitions from the Thinking Economy to the Feeling Economy. In other words, we predict that more advanced economies should feature more women in positions of influence and authority.

To provide some preliminary descriptive evidence of this, let us consider the top 10 best nations for women, as compiled by US News.[12] If our thesis is correct, these countries should be at the forefront of economic progress as the economy moves into the Feeling Economy, and women assume greater influence. These nations are Denmark, Sweden, the Netherlands, Norway, Canada, Finland, Switzerland, New Zealand, Australia, and Austria. Those women-forward countries range in per capita GDP from about $40,000 to about $75,000, with a median of about $52,000. This compares to an average global GDP per capita of about $17,000, indicating that the top countries for women are also high achievers economically. This should be increasingly the case as the Feeling Economy develops. It is also worth noting that Europe's biggest economy, Germany, is led by a woman, Angela Merkel, as are four of the top 10 countries on the best nations for women list. The Feeling Economy should bring even more female leaders into power.

With the world increasingly feeling-oriented as AI advances, it makes sense that leaders who can mix intelligence and empathy should be poised to succeed. This idea was tested in the coronavirus crisis of 2020, in which women leaders from New Zealand, Norway, Iceland, Germany, and Taiwan earned high marks for their stewardship of the crisis. New Zealand's Prime Minister, Jacinda Ardern, enacted tough mitigation procedures, but also demonstrated emotional intelligence. For example, she streamed videos of herself and family at home, and announced that the tooth fairy and Easter Bunny were "essential workers." About Ardern, the *Washington Post* wrote, "She often emphasizes empathy in her public remarks, demonstrating …that one 'can actually lead with both resolve and kindness."[13] Such an approach contrasts strongly with the hyper-masculine style assumed by Donald Trump, Vladimir Putin, and numerous strongmen around the world.

There is evidence that women are assuming a higher percentage of the growth jobs in the Feeling Economy. As mentioned in Chapter 6, such jobs are more likely to be in the healthcare, medical, and managerial fields. Fields like nursing have traditionally been dominated by women. Doctors, who in many countries have traditionally more often been men, are now seeing more women entering their ranks. For example, in 2019, the Association of American Medical Colleges reported that women now make up the majority of US medical students, for the first time.[14] The same thing is starting to happen in the managerial realm. The US Bureau of Labor Statistics reports that 37% of managerial jobs are now held by women, and that percentage is certain to increase. While in 2005, none of the leading business schools enrolled more than 40% women, today there are many such schools, including Harvard, Wharton, and MIT.

Conclusions

Throughout history, men's unique strengths have set them up to be the dominant players in the economy. From the Physical Economy, which valued men's physical strength, to the Thinking Economy, which values men's mathematical and spatial abilities, men have always had an advantage. That advantage was further solidified by inertia, as male-dominant social structures have given way only grudgingly.

The Feeling Economy turns all of this on its head. Because empathy, emotion, feelings, and interpersonal skills (traditionally women's strengths) are assuming unprecedented importance, an era of women seems likely to emerge. We already see that the societies that embrace this shift the most, and give more power to women, are economically more successful, and more likely to have women leaders.

Although women have advanced considerably in the Thinking Economy, there is still a wage gap in most advanced economies. We can anticipate that this wage gap will continue to decline, and in fact may reverse, as women assume greater power and influence in the economy. Just as many women have needed to be "more like men" in the Thinking Economy, focusing on STEM skills and systematic reasoning, men who wish to be successful in the Feeling Economy may need to focus on their feminine side, and become better at the traditional women's strengths of empathy and interpersonal relationships. To paraphrase (and reverse) the great soul singer, James Brown, "It's a woman's world." He is probably spinning in his grave as we enter the Feeling Economy.

Notes

1. *Infoplease* (2019), "Women's Suffrage: When and Where Did Women Earn the Right to Vote?" www.infoplease.com/history/womens-history/womens-suffrage, accessed October 30, 2019.
2. Cox, Jeff (2019), "Stephen Moore Says the Decline in 'Male Earnings' Is a Big Issue for the Economy," www.cnbc.com, accessed October 30, 2019.
3. AAUW (2020), "The Simple Truth about the Gender Pay Gap," https://www.aauw.org/research/the-simple-truth-about-the-gender-pay-gap/, accessed January 21, 2020.
4. *Time* (2020), *The Science of Gender*, Single Issue Magazine, January 31, 2020.
5. Becker, Gary S. (1957), *The Economics of Discrimination*, Chicago: University of Chicago Press.

6. Phelps, Edmund S. (1972), "The Statistical Theory of Racism and Sexism," *American Economic Review*, 62 (4), 659–661.
7. Ukanwa, Kalinda, and Roland T. Rust (2020), "Discrimination in Service," Working Paper, University of Maryland.
8. Telford, Taylor (2019), "Apple Card Scrutinized for Alleged Gender Disparities," *Washington Post*, November 12, A22.
9. Xin, Jiang, Yaoxue Zhang, Yan Tang, and Yuan Yang (2019), "Brain Differences between Men and Women: Evidence from Deep Learning," *Frontiers in Neuroscience*, March 8, accessed at https://www.frontiersin.org/articles/10.3389/fnins.2019.00185/full on April 7, 2020.
10. Perez, Caroline Criado (2020), "Closing the Gender Data Gap," *Time*, February 3, 80–81,
11. Greenberg, David M., Varun Warrier, Carrie Allison, and Simon Baron-Cohen (2018), "Testing the Empathizing-Systemizing Theory of Sex Differences and the Extreme Male Brain Theory of Autism in Half a Million People," *PNAS*, 115 (48), 12152–12157.
12. U.S. News (2020), "Best Countries for Women," accessed at https://www.usnews.com/news/best-countries/best-women on January 21, 2020.
13. O'Grady, Siobhan, and Jennifer Hassan (2020), "Female World Leaders Hailed as Voices of Reason amid Coronavirus Chaos," *Washington Post*, April 21, A13.
14. Association of American Medical Colleges (2019), "The Majority of U.S. Medical Students Are Women, New Data Show," accessed at https://www.aamc.org/news-insights/press-releases/majority-us-medical-students-are-women-new-data-show on April 7, 2020.

8

Politics That Feel

As people increasingly delegate their thinking tasks to AI based in the Internet and accessible by smartphones and digital assistants, their thinking abilities atrophy. This means that the best way to reach people is now through their emotions. As a result, as the electorate becomes more feeling-oriented, political campaigns and political candidates are also becoming more feeling-oriented.

How AI Transforms Media

Increased capabilities with respect to the communication, storage, and analysis of information has made possible a dramatic expansion of media vehicles. Whereas in the United States, there used to be no more than three or four available TV channels, now (including cable, Internet, and live streaming) there are thousands of available options. AI can then analyze viewing information at the individual level, and personalize advertising. The circulations of traditional print media (e.g., newspapers and magazines) are dramatically declining as the electronic options proliferate.[1]

The Canadian media philosopher Marshall McLuhan notes that how people interact with a medium is mostly a function of the medium itself.[2] He sorts media into "cool" media that demand more user participation, and "hot" media that don't require the user to fill in as many details. With "cool" print media giving way to "hot" electronic ones, the thinking that the reader used to do is, to a fair degree, replaced by feeling. Thus, the nature

© The Author(s) 2021
R. T. Rust and M.-H. Huang, *The Feeling Economy*,
https://doi.org/10.1007/978-3-030-52977-2_8

of electronic media reinforce the tendency toward less thinking and more feeling.

Rush Limbaugh and Talk Radio

An early adoptee of feeling-based political discourse was Rush Limbaugh. Whereas previous political commentators (e.g., Walter Cronkite) mostly sought to be factual and present political information as news, Limbaugh instead portrays himself as a conservative advocate with clear (and somewhat extreme) political views. His radio programs seek mostly to present arguments from primarily an emotional basis. He seeks not only to build up those with similar views but also to ridicule his political opponents. The Presidency of Donald Trump is seen by some commentators as the logical extension of Limbaugh's emotional approach.[3]

Fox News

Fox News was created by media magnate Rupert Murdoch and TV executive Roger Ailes, in 1996. Fox News calls itself "fair and balanced," but in truth reflects a consistently conservative viewpoint. The network is positioned counter to the traditional broadcast networks (e.g., ABC, CBS, and NBC), in that it has a clear political viewpoint. As a result, some of Fox News' competitor networks (e.g., CNN and MSNBC) have moved to the left, to provide a political counterweight to Fox. Fox News remains somewhat controversial, and many of its "hard news" staff have left. The focus of Fox News is now on its commentators, such as Sean Hannity, Laura Ingraham, and Tucker Carlson. Those commentators, like Rush Limbaugh on radio, adopt primarily emotional arguments, to try to get their base fired up. President Donald Trump is a perfect fit with the network, due to his conservative views and emotional style.

Social Media

Social media such as Facebook claim to exist to bring people together, but their business models are typically based on online advertising, the more personalized the better. AI provides the computational capability to target advertising more and more finely. The ability to personalize advertising further motivates media to provide even more fragmented offerings, so that even more precise targeting can be obtained. Unfortunately, this also encourages more extreme views,[4] as well as the "echo chamber" effect. Extreme content that can stir emotions generates the highest levels of reposting, so that is what the social media encourage and promote, either explicitly or implicitly. The result is that social media are a reverberating system in which news stories, corporate communications, and individual posts all affect each other.[5]

Bad actors use AI to transform not just social media, but also the content that appears on social media. AI-driven bots can create large numbers of fake communications that can be used to manipulate unwary voters. AI is now also being used to alter photos and videos in a way that most people cannot detect. All of this AI-generated mischief can be used to try to manipulate elections, as the Russians demonstrated in the 2016 US elections.[6]

The Voting Process

Voting involves two main steps: (1) deciding to register and vote, and (2) voting. With voters now thinking less and feeling more, the tasks of political marketing become (a) get your side to register and vote, (b) discourage the other side from registering and voting, and (c) encourage voters to vote for your side. Task a) can be seen as "firing up your base." Emotional arguments can motivate your own voters (either to vote *for* your side, or vote *against* the other side). Task b) can be seen as "voter suppression." For example, Republicans may target black voters by saying the Democrats are taking them for granted, and therefore they should send a message and not vote. Task c) is the conventional persuasion task, but it is less important in the era of personalized communications. The political advertiser already has a pretty good idea how each person would vote, so the key becomes turnout, and emotion is the key to turnout.

Donald Trump

It seems strange to say that Donald Trump, hated by many and the most divisive President in recent years, owes his success to the Feeling Economy. Nevertheless, that is the case. In the 2016 campaign, Trump realized that there were many people in the battleground states in the Midwest who felt left behind by the decline of the Physical Economy. These were people who may formerly have enjoyed high-paying manufacturing jobs, or perhaps were farmers or coal miners. Trump focused on those people's discontent, and sold it back to them. Meanwhile Trump (and the Russians who were attempting to aid him) also did everything he could to discourage Democrats from voting. As an example, there was a serious effort to turn Bernie Sanders' supporters against Democratic nominee, Hillary Clinton.[7] AI analysis of social media data was used to focus this effort.

The same strategy was used by Trump and his supporters when promoting Brett Kavanaugh for the Supreme Court. The primary witness against Kavanaugh, Christine Blasey Ford, provided a very compelling, emotional testimony. Rather than address Dr. Ford's testimony directly, the Republicans adopted a different strategy. Senator Lindsay Graham, followed by others, spoke directly and emotionally to the Republican base, literally shouting down the other side, including the introverted Dr. Ford.

A similar strategy was effectively used by the Republicans in the impeachment trial of Donald Trump. The Republicans essentially ignored the Democrats' charges, and instead spoke directly and emotionally to Trump and his base of supporters. Once again, the Republicans used raised voices and emotionally loaded words (e.g., "hoax," "sham") to make an emotional case rather than a rational one. Thus, even though the facts of the case were not really in doubt, the Republicans could still win the day by making an emotional argument that would stimulate people's prejudices and instinctive disapproval of the other side.

Ironically, the Feeling Economy winds that swept Trump into office may also be his undoing. At the time of this writing, the world has been plunged into a coronavirus pandemic, and Trump has shown a remarkable inability to express empathy. Republican columnist Michael Gerson, writing in the *Washington Post*, said, "Trump seems incapable of imagining and reflecting the fears, suffering and grief of his fellow citizens. We have witnessed the total failure of empathy in presidential leadership." Although he is still favored to be re-elected at the time of this writing (May 2020), based on the nature of the Feeling Economy, we predict difficulties for him in the upcoming Presidential election.

The Clintons

The Clintons are an outstanding example of both how to utilize politics that feel, and how not to utilize them. Even though he was impeached while in office, Bill Clinton left office as one of the most popular Presidents in history. He famously said once that "I feel your pain," and that emotional connection inoculated him against any negative political winds, including even lying to the Congress.

By contrast, his wife, Hillary, did not show much ability to make an emotional connection with voters. Friends would often urge her to open up and show her humanity, but her public person was always cold and analytic—something that used to work, but is not an effective strategy in the Feeling Economy. She might have overcome this by making greater use of her husband, who has always had a strong ability to relate to people, in the campaign.

Bernie Sanders

Along with Elizabeth Warren, Bernie Sanders created a compelling vision of change that galvanized progressive voters nationally. Nevertheless, Sanders was not a good fit for the Feeling Economy, and this was one of the main reasons that he lost. Ahead in the primaries, and seemingly steaming toward the Democratic nomination, Sanders' personal qualities eventually doomed him. As Rachel Manteuffel, who followed Sanders' campaign, wrote in the *Washington Post* magazine about one encounter that Sanders had with a sick, uninsured man[8]:

> He juggles numbers nimbly but isn't, it seemed clear, quite sure what to do with emotions. It was perhaps the moment for a hug, but Bernie couldn't quite go there. He extended his long arm to Ryan's shoulder and simultaneously shook his hand, without getting any closer. Literally, this became an arm's length transaction.

In other words, for all his ideas and evident compassion for the less fortunate, Sanders has an empathy problem, and it was his downfall.

Joe Biden

Joe Biden was not the smartest Democrat in the 2020 Presidential race. He was prone to gaffes, and many of his utterances caused people to question his mental acuity. His Democratic debate performances were mediocre, at best. What Biden does have, though, is empathy. "Uncle Joe" really cares about his fellow man (and woman), and people tend to trust him. He does not have to pretend to care, and people notice.

Similar to Donald Trump and Bill Clinton, Joe Biden has a natural tendency to relate to people on a feeling basis. In fact, his tendency to put his arm around people has almost gotten him in trouble. That same tendency for emotional connection also gives Biden a degree of protection. When he messes up a statement or does poorly in a debate, people tend to forgive "Uncle Joe." Like Trump, Biden also comes across as fallible and human. Once, when a supporter asked him about Hunter Biden's controversial appointment at Burisma in Ukraine, Joe Biden snapped back, "You're a liar, man!" Again, people immediately forgave Biden, because they feel they have an emotional relationship with him. When the COVID-19 crisis hit, Biden was strongly in his element, giving a speech to the nation as "comforter in chief."

It is not an accident that Biden, known for his age, mental fuzziness, and gaffes, drove seemingly smarter and better prepared candidates, such as Elizabeth Warren and Pete Buttigieg, out of the Presidential race. They simply were not as warm as Biden, who people can relate to emotionally. At the time of this writing, Biden is strongly in command of the Democratic nomination, and our guess is that his more authentic version of empathy will cause Donald Trump a lot of problems in the 2020 US Presidential election.[9] Although Trump still is favored in the betting markets at the time of this writing (May 2020), we predict that the rising importance of empathy will favor Biden. As the *Washington Post* notes, Trump's biggest Achilles heel (sorry) is the empathy gap.[10]

Brexit and Boris Johnson

The United Kingdom has also seen the effectiveness of an emotional approach to politics. The Brexit movement began as more of a symbolic expression of hate toward the European Union and the immigration that the EU supported. The arguments in favor of Brexit were not well-reasoned, and a high percentage of the more educated and higher income people did not support it. Nevertheless, there were enough rural, uneducated people who felt left out by the changing economy, and Brexit was passed. Similar to Trump, the United Kingdom had a charismatic, yellow-haired advocate. Although seen as a bit of an intellectual lightweight, Boris Johnson knew how to connect to the public emotionally, and that was why he won.

The European Right

Populism in Europe does not end with the United Kingdom. Many of the same issues that drove Brexit (e.g., immigration, unemployment, lack of opportunity) have created an opening for emotional arguments of the "us vs. them" type. Far right, anti-immigration parties have made major gains in such countries as Hungary, Austria, Germany, and Italy. Demagogues thrive under changing conditions that lend themselves to easy emotional arguments and scapegoating, and this is a time of expansion for the populist right in Europe.

Conclusions

AI promotes politics that feel for two reasons. It changes the nature of the media we attend to, by making media more fragmented and personalized. In addition, AI makes it easier to manipulate emotions by facilitating fake news and doctored images and videos.[11]

The movement toward the Feeling Economy has presented politicians with new opportunities. Populist politicians who can divide the population by firing up people's emotions are on the rise all over the world. Campaign strategies are evolving from logical arguments to emotional persuasion. Thus, we now see successful politicians with limited factual knowledge or coherent strategy, but with the ability to empathize (or pretend to empathize) with the populace. As the Feeling Economy advances, this emotional approach to politics is likely to become more widespread.

Notes

1. Watson, Amy (2019), "US Print Media Industry: Statistics & Facts," *Statista*, accessed at https://www.statista.com/topics/1052/print-media/ on January 22, 2020.
2. McLuhan, Marshall (1964), *Understanding Media: The Extensions of Man*, New York: McGraw-Hill.
3. Rosenwald, Brian (2019), *Talk Radio's America: How an Industry Took Over a Political Party that Took Over the United States*, Cambridge, MA: Harvard University Press.
4. Kozinets, Robert (2017), "How Social Media Fires Peoples' Passions— And Builds Extremist Divisions," *The Conversation*, November 13, accessed

at http://theconversation.com/how-social-media-fires-peoples-passions-and-bui lds-extremist-divisions-86909 on January 22, 2020.

5. Hewett, Kelly, William Rand, Roland T. Rust and Harald J. van Heerde (2016), "Brand Buzz in the Echoverse," *Journal of Marketing*, 80 (3), 1–24.

6. Abrams, Abigail (2019), "Here's What We Know So Far about Russia's 2016 Meddling," *Time*, accessed at https://time.com/5565991/russia-influence-2016-election/ on January 22, 2020.

7. Marcin, Tim (2018), "Russian 2016 Election Influence Tried to Suppress Votes of Bernie Sanders Supporters, African-Americans, Report Finds," *Newsweek*, December 17, accessed at https://www.newsweek.com/russia-2016-election-ber nie-sanders-trump-1261425 on January 22, 2020.

8. Manteuffel, Rachel (2020), "The Heart of Bernie Sanders," *Washington Post Magazine*, March 29, 22–31.

9. Blake, Aaron (2020), "Trump's Biggest Deficit against Biden: Empathy," *Washington Post*, accessed at https://www.washingtonpost.com/politics/2020/05/22/ trumps-biggest-deficit-against-biden-empathy/ on May 29, 2020.

10. Gerson, Michael (2020), "An Empathy Shortage," *Washington Post*, April 3, A23.

11. Schwartz, Oscar (2018), "You Thought Fake News Was Bad? Deep Fakes Are Where Truth Goes to Die," *The Guardian*, November 12, accessed at https:// www.theguardian.com/technology/2018/nov/12/deep-fakes-fake-news-truth on January 22, 2020.

9

How Education Must Change

The current educational system is designed to produce Thinking Economy workers. That has not always been true, and it will soon not be true again. The Physical Economy emphasized very different skills. When the Physical Economy was superseded by the Thinking Economy, the educational system was forced to adapt. A similar adaptation is required today, as the Feeling Economy begins to overtake the Thinking Economy. Skills that are highly prized today may soon be worth much less, which suggests the need for a revolution in education. In the Feeling Economy, the most prized skills are likely to be empathy, emotional intelligence,[1] communication, and interpersonal relationships. This will require a different kind of education. Many of today's Thinking Economy workers will be faced with a massive dislocation, as the skills they need to compete change to Feeling Economy skills. This suggests a heightened need for retraining and continuing education.

Education in the Physical Economy

We are accustomed to thinking of education as something that happens to people in schools, but for a very long time the most important education occurred outside of schools. The churches were largely responsible for moral education, but education specific to everyday work life was mostly accomplished through apprenticeships, if skills were required. If the work was unskilled, then children were often just put to work at a young age. As a result, it was commonplace to see children working long hours on the farm, in the factory, or in the mines, doing physically demanding jobs. Education,

© The Author(s) 2021
R. T. Rust and M.-H. Huang, *The Feeling Economy*,
https://doi.org/10.1007/978-3-030-52977-2_9

such as it was, involved learning just enough to accomplish the necessary physical tasks.

As a result, much of the learning in the Physical Economy related to muscle memory, manual dexterity, and physical strength. There was a small elite that focused on thinking skills such as mathematics, philosophy, reading, and writing, but they tended to be the royalty or the priesthood. Most early universities arose out of religious orders, and their primary purpose was to train the priesthood. The idea of universal education, in the modern sense, is a relatively recent phenomenon. For example, in the year 1870 in the United States, only 2% of the population graduated from high school.[2] Given the nature of the Physical Economy, this lack of attention to thinking skills was not a huge detriment to society.

The Current Approach: Education in the Thinking Economy

As the Thinking Economy arose, which mostly coincided with the Industrial Revolution, more than just the elites needed to be able to solve nontrivial mental problems. The society now needed such people as engineers, accountants, and lawyers, as the largely agrarian Physical Economy gave way to a more urban Thinking Economy, with far more complex organizations and technologies, and a much more rapid pace of change.

The central, and mostly unquestioned, assumption of the Thinking Economy is that the purpose of education is to teach people to think. This takes more years to teach, due to the complexity of what is taught. For example, an engineer might need to know and use calculus, but before calculus, he/she would typically learn algebra and geometry, and before that, simple arithmetic. The result is that as the Thinking Economy has advanced, the length of education has increased. For example, the percentage of the US population that receive a high school education increased from 2% in the year 1870 to 77% in the year 1969.[3] The percentage with four years or more of college increased from less than 5% in 1940 to about 35% today.[4]

Thinking Economy education works. The technical ability of Thinking Economy workers has increased immensely in the last 200 years. We can see the evidence of this anywhere. Compare the quality of medical care today to the medical care of 100 years ago. Consider the many impressive inventions and technological achievements that have arisen just in the last 150 years. Workers educated to be thinkers created automobiles, airplanes, computers, smartphones, television, radio, rockets to the moon (and beyond), antibiotics, and the Internet. The very success of Thinking Economy education makes it almost impossible to imagine that such an education can possibly be wrong. Nevertheless, we conclude that the Thinking Economy education is increasingly obsolete.

Why Thinking Economy Education Fails in the Feeling Economy

Consider a company that wishes to hire a computer programmer. Let us suppose there are two candidates—Programmer A and Programmer B. Suppose that Programmer A is more capable and/or cheaper than Programmer B. There can be little doubt in such a case that the company will hire Programmer A. Now consider what is happening today, with the increasing capability of artificial intelligence. In many situations such as the previous one, Candidate A might be AI, and Candidate B might be human. In such a case, there can be little doubt that the company would use AI to do the job that might formerly have been done by humans.

In real life, things are a little bit more complicated. Most jobs involve a variety of tasks. For some of those tasks, AI is likely to be better, and for other tasks, humans (HI) are likely to be better. In such a case, the company may employ AI to do the tasks for which it is superior, and employ HI to do the tasks for which it is superior. The problem is that it is exactly the thinking tasks for which AI is ideally suited. As we document elsewhere in the book AI is rapidly increasing its ability to perform difficult thinking tasks. For example, AI can already beat the best human players in complex games such as Chess and Go. It can also often outperform humans in such things as medical diagnosis.

What this all means is that students who continue to focus on the same thinking skills that AI is getting good at are essentially beating their heads against a brick wall. They would be better focusing on those skills that AI has a harder time with. That, in turn, requires a different kind of education.

Educational Transitions

We have seen this kind of educational transition before. The first wave of automation was essentially physical. Instead of humans building cars by hand, cars were built on an assembly line. This put many of the factory workers out of work. A similar dislocation occurred on farms and in mines, both of which became more mechanized. The result was a large number of physical workers with under-developed thinking skills who were unprepared for the job market in the Thinking Economy. In the United States today, we can see many manufacturing regions (think Ohio, Indiana, Pennsylvania, or Wisconsin) that vainly hope for a return of manufacturing jobs. Unscrupulous politicians (please forgive the redundancy) typically promise that their party will be the one to bring those jobs back. The sad truth is that those jobs are *not* coming back, and the solution to the problem is a different kind of education. Many physical workers need retraining to compete in the current economy. However, with the economy now moving to the Feeling Economy, even the thinking skills, that can help a worker compete today, may be the wrong thing for tomorrow.

STEM Skills—A Dead End?

In the Thinking Economy, the most valued skills are STEM skills. The acronym, STEM, stands for science, technology, engineering, and mathematics. These skills are in short supply in the Thinking Economy, with many jobs that require STEM skills going unfilled. It is projected that there are as many as 2.4 million unfilled STEM jobs in the United States, many of them well-paying.[5] Information technology companies, in particular, find it difficult to hire as many qualified people as they need. The supply of US-based STEM-qualified people is insufficient, which has led to a desire by that industry to attract qualified immigrants, mostly from India. At the same time, US government immigration regulations limit the number of immigrants that can be brought in from any one country. The result is that an Indian immigrant on an H1B visa (the one appropriate for STEM-based immigrants) can expect to be on a waiting list for as long as 150 years, according to the Cato Institute.[6]

All of this may lead one to conclude that STEM skills are the key to a good job, and education should emphasize STEM skills much more. We heartily acknowledge that STEM skills are, in fact, currently in great demand, and that people in STEM jobs earn attractive salaries. The first author (Rust) was trained in mathematics, and has found those skills to be invaluable in his job as a college business professor. It is ironic, therefore, that we conclude that STEM skills may soon be worse much less, and that the importance of STEM skills is already declining.

The advance of artificial intelligence increasingly enables computing to emulate most or all of the STEM skills that are valued so highly today. As a result, as the Feeling Economy develops, having STEM skills will no longer be valued as much as it is today. Human workers will then have to develop skills that *complement* the STEM skills that will increasingly be delegated to AI. Already, there are calls for STEM workers to expand their capabilities beyond just the core STEM skills.[7]

Some analysts already conclude that STEM skills may no longer be enough. Mitchell Baker, the Chair and Co-Founder of Mozilla, presented some contrary opinions at the annual STEM summit. She concludes that STEM workers must be trained more broadly, to focus more on how STEM jobs affect people and the whole of society. The Rhode Island School of Design champions an idea called STEAM, which adds the acronym for "arts" to the STEM skills.[8] This recommendation responds to an intermediate stage in the development of the Feeling Economy. As we have discussed previously, thinking skills may be broken down into analytical skills (relatively easier for AI to emulate) and intuitive skills (relatively harder for AI). For the intermediate stage in which it is mostly the analytical skills that are being addressed by AI, humans can stay relevant by somewhat deemphasizing the core STEM skills (which are inherently analytical) and paying more attention to the creative, artistic, and intuitive skills. Thus, the "A" skills become more important.

Ultimately, though, all of the STEM skills are at risk from AI, which will force the workforce to develop the people skills that the Feeling Economy will require. This is already beginning to happen. Even leading tech companies are finding that STEM skills are not enough. Google, for example, in a rigorous study of its HR data, found that of the eight top skills associated with Google employees' jobs, STEM skills came in last.[9] More important, already, were almost all "soft" people skills. This is the direction that education must head.

Education in the Feeling Economy

In the Feeling Economy, the emphasis of education needs to move toward the softer people skills. Such skills include empathy, emotional intelligence, communication, interpersonal relationships, and coaching and leadership. It is likely to take decades before AI can successfully compete with humans in these areas.

Consider the nature of many school environments today. Students file into a room with several dozen (or even hundreds) of other students, and passively listen to lectures. Occasionally, perhaps, they have the opportunity to raise their hand and answer a question. Many students are completely passive throughout the class period, perhaps writing notes, or perhaps just spending time on their smartphones, texting and surfing the Web. Back at home or in their dorm rooms, they read textbooks. Perhaps they write reports occasionally, but often the only communication they initiate is filling out a multiple-choice exam. Such an education does not begin to prepare a student for the Feeling Economy.

A Feeling Economy education would look a lot different. Currently, many college students get more Feeling Economy education in their dormitory, fraternity, or sorority than they do in their classes. If people skills are of primary importance, then having students interact with each other is essential. The first author (Rust) addresses this need in several different ways in the college classes that he teaches:

1. Students work in groups. Even quiet students need to learn how to function more forcefully and effectively in an interpersonal environment, and overbearing students need to learn when to back off. Differences of opinion or differences of background force students to understand and appreciate perspectives that are different from their own. Students are forced to develop more empathy and emotional intelligence in such an environment.
2. Students develop coaching and leadership skills. People who have natural leadership skills need to learn when those skills are needed, and how best to exercise them. When Rust was an MBA student at the University of North Carolina, he was the youngest person in the program, with most of his peers being much older and more experienced. Although Rust had natural leadership skills, it took some time to realize that sometimes the group needed those skills, and that he needed to assert them for the group to be effective. Without group work, he would not have learned how to do that.
3. Students give group presentations. Effective oral presentations are essential to interact effectively in an organizational environment. Also, the group nature of the presentations further facilitates give and take with the others in the group. Group decision dynamics are actively practiced in such a setting.
4. Students have frequent group written assignments. As in the group presentations, this also develops the skills necessary to function effectively in a group. This also helps develop the student's written communication skills, which are often poorly developed in the current educational environment.

In summary, the nature of Feeling Economy education is far more people-oriented. Of course, when one aspect is emphasized more, other aspects need to be emphasized less. In the case of Feeling Economy education, the aspects receiving less emphasis will be the technical aspects—the STEM skills that are more at risk of being taken over by AI.

Retraining Thinking Economy Workers

Consider the stereotypical Silicon Valley geek, the narrowly technical, socially awkward person made fun of in the TV shows, *Silicon Valley* and *The Big Bang Theory*. As we have seen previously in this chapter, this stereotype is already mostly obsolete, even in Silicon Valley. To be successful, even in a tech company such as Google, a worker needs to be adept interpersonally. The tensions this creates for the pure STEM worker are dramatized brilliantly in Ethan Canin's bestselling novel, *A Doubter's Almanac*. In that book, the brilliant but socially toxic mathematician fades to oblivion, while his less brilliant, but more socially adept, department chair is professionally successful. The STEM stars will need to be retrained to be able to compete successfully in the Feeling Economy, and this need will only intensify as the Feeling Economy develops.

This calls for continuing education to play an important role. Although the society has largely failed in retraining Physical Economy workers to become Thinking Economy workers, it is essential that we do better in the transition from the Thinking Economy to the Feeling Economy. Universities can play a major role in this retraining, which suggests the importance of new or expanded programs, targeted at STEM workers, and mostly focused on "soft" people skills.

Conclusions

The Feeling Economy will turn education on its head, replacing the current unquestioned emphasis on thinking skills with an emphasis on feeling skills and interpersonal skills. This will also require an increasing attention to continuing education, to help technical workers to become more well-rounded and better able to interact with others. Group work and a focus on communication skills are a must. Topics like empathy and emotional intelligence will become central.

Notes

1. Goleman, Daniel (1995), *Emotional Intelligence: Why It Can Matter More than IQ*, New York: Bantam Books.
2. *Education Week*, accessed on April 9, 2020 at https://www.edweek.org/media/34gradrate-c1.pdf.
3. *Education Week*, op. cit.
4. *Statista* (2020), "Percentage of the U.S. Population Who Have Completed Four Years of College or More from 1940 to 2019, by Gender," accessed at https://www.statista.com/statistics/184272/educational-attainment-of-college-diploma-or-higher-by-gender/ on April 9, 2020.
5. Smithsonian Science Education Center (2020), "The STEM Imperative," accessed at https://ssec.si.edu/stem-imperative on January 30, 2020.
6. Cato Institute (2018), "15-Year Wait for Indian Immigrants with Advanced Degrees," accessed at https://www.cato.org/blog/150-year-wait-indian-immigrants-advanced-degrees on April 9, 2020.
7. Baker, Mitchell (2019), "How STEM Education Must Evolve," *Scientific American*, accessed at https://blogs.scientificamerican.com/observations/how-stem-education-must-evolve/ on January 30, 2020.
8. Marr, Bernard (2020), "We Need STEAM, Not STEM Education, To Prepare Our Kids for the 4th Industrial Revolution," *Forbes*, accessed at https://www.forbes.com/sites/bernardmarr/2020/01/15/we-need-steam-not-stem-education-to-prepare-our-kids-for-the-4th-industrial-revolution/#5d72f6b355fb on January 30, 2020.
9. Strauss, Valerie (2017), "The Surprising Thing Google Learned About Its Employees—And What It Means for Todays' Students," *Washington Post*, accessed at https://www.washingtonpost.com/news/answer-sheet/wp/2017/12/20/the-surprising-thing-google-learned-about-its-employees-and-what-it-means-for-todays-students/ on January 30, 2020.

10

AI for Consumers

Many people think of AI as a tool that businesses employ, and of course business actually is applying AI very widely. However, consumers also use AI, and it is having a profound impact on how regular people live their lives. What's more, AI is changing people's very nature in a systematic way. Consumers in an AI-dominant world are very different from the consumers of previous generations. This chapter first discusses the three intelligence levels of AI, and gives examples of how mechanical AI, thinking AI and feeling AI are (or will be) addressing consumer needs. Mechanical AI is already quite widespread, and its implications are already mostly manifest. Thinking AI is where the greatest change is taking place today. Examples of feeling AI already exist, but feeling AI's most significant impact is still in the future. After exploring the many ways in which consumers are using (or will be using) AI, we then focus on the changing consumer—how the consumer who uses AI is being profoundly changed by that collaboration.

Mechanical AI for Consumers

Mechanical AI is so prosaic and well-entrenched that we don't usually think of it as AI. Examples of mechanical AI for consumers mostly tend to be applications that replace human physical effort, or that let a machine take over repetitive or monotonous tasks. To clarify what it is, and what it does, we explore several common examples. There are many, many such examples, but the following should be suggestive of what mechanical AI can do for consumers.

© The Author(s) 2021
R. T. Rust and M.-H. Huang, *The Feeling Economy*,
https://doi.org/10.1007/978-3-030-52977-2_10

One example used by many consumers is automatic braking systems (ABS). Before ABS, consumers driving in snowy or slick conditions were taught to "pump" the brakes—braking, then backing off, then braking, then backing off, etc., in rapid succession. The purpose is to keep the brakes from locking up. This requires a lot of physical strength and coordination. The ABS system does this automatically. If the brakes are applied, and the conditions are sufficiently slick, then the ABS system pumps the brakes automatically, and much faster than a typical driver is capable of. This helps keep the car going straight on the road, and reduces the probability of a dangerous skid.

People suffering from heart arrhythmia have a heartbeat that is too slow, too fast, or too irregular. For example, atrial fibrillation is a heart arrhythmia condition that may be quite dangerous. Left untreated, heart arrhythmia may result in a variety of negative results, such as stroke or heart failure. To address this, doctors often install pacemakers to govern the heart's rhythm. Although pacemakers create some undesirable restrictions (e.g., it may be impossible to do intense physical exercise that would require a fast heartbeat), they typically get the arrhythmia under control and let the consumer live a normal life.

Almost everyone uses an alarm clock of some sort, but few would think of it as AI. That's what it is, however. The alarm clock keeps track of the time, to a degree that would be very difficult for most people, and then wakes up the user at the appropriate time. This is a repetitive and monotonous task, but AI can do it very well.

Washing and drying the dishes is a tedious task when done by hand, which has led to automatic dishwashers becoming a popular consumer appliance. The device chooses the right water temperature, rinses the dishes, washes them with detergent, and then dries them, all at the right time. Similarly, electronic clothes washers and driers are ubiquitous today. Consumers who don't own those appliances may easily use them on a rental basis at a local laundromat.

Vacuuming the floor is a household chore that takes time and effort. The Roomba vacuum does this automatically, freeing consumers for other tasks, and enabling even physically disabled people to take care of their floors.

Mechanical AI was the first AI application for consumers, and it is already well-established.

Thinking AI for Consumers

Thinking AI is the type that is advancing most rapidly today. The purpose of thinking AI for consumers is to assume some of the thinking tasks that consumers may not want to do, or are not capable of doing. The following are some common examples.

Today, *Statista* estimates that there are 3.5 billion smartphones in existence in 2020.[1] Such phones are not just phones. By connecting online, a consumer can easily do difficult mathematical calculations that would be impossible for most people in their head. They can also use search engines to find and choose the most relevant websites to address particular queries. Other interfaces, such as Amazon's Echo, can also provide such help.

Digital assistants are everywhere today. From Apple's Siri, to Google Assistant, to Amazon's Alexa, Samsung's Bixby, and Microsoft's Cortana, digital assistants can help with a wide variety of tasks, including such things as answering questions, ordering supplies, controlling the home electronics, and an almost endless list of other capabilities, some of which have not even been thought of yet.[2] As time goes by, these digital assistants become more understanding of such things as context, and can do a better job of personalization.

GPS navigation systems, such as Waze and Google Maps, simplify the difficult navigation task of finding destinations, even if the consumer has never been to those destinations before. What used to be a pre-trip ritual of using physical maps to map out a route now can be done in real time by AI.

Word processing is another popular AI application. Email software, for example, will often spell check and make suggestions about grammar. Some apps will even draft replies to simple queries. Such applications save the consumer time, and also make it somewhat less important for consumers to have perfect spelling and grammar.

Netflix provides another thinking AI example. Figuring out which movie to watch can be a daunting challenge, given the many thousands of potential options. To address this problem, Netflix uses sophisticated algorithms to recommend movies that will match a user's past behavior and revealed preferences. Searching through and analyzing all relevant options would be too time-consuming for any individual consumer. Similar recommendation algorithms are also used by applications in many other areas, such as networking (e.g., LinkedIn), music (e.g., Pandora), and news (e.g., Google News).

One emerging technology for thinking AI is augmented reality (AR). Popularized by the ill-fated Google Glass (whose wearers were often branded "Glassholes" for invading people's privacy), plus start-ups like Oculus, AR, connected online, has the knowledge and computing power of a smartphone, combined with the ability to project the information visually. For example, a consumer walking down a street might learn all the shopping options available in that geographic location, or even (potentially) recognize by face anyone they meet.

Thinking AI applications are proliferating rapidly, and as AI develops more thinking intelligence, we can expect considerable growth in these kinds of applications.

Feeling AI for Consumers

Feeling AI for consumers is not as far along, but it also has considerable future potential. Such applications seek to meet some of the consumer's social and relationship needs. This is especially important for groups of people with fewer social connections, such as many lonely older people. Feeling AI applications tend to focus on social connections and interpersonal relationships. The following are some feeling AI examples that already exist.

One early example of this was ELIZA, which was an AI natural language therapist, devised by Joseph Weizenbaum of MIT's AI lab in the 1960s. ELIZA had only the most rudimentary cognitive ability, and mostly just recycled words that the patient had typed in, adding some encouraging comments and asking for the patient to expand. The interesting finding was that many patients developed strong feelings toward ELIZA, as though the program were a person. This illustrated that feeling AI does not have to be perfect to be effective. Humans naturally project consciousness onto such social applications.

Loneliness is a huge problem for many people. For example, many young Japanese men find it difficult to attract a wife, leading to an important unmet need. The Japanese company Gatebox has addressed this need by building a holographic "wife" named Aizuma Hikari. She can talk to her owner on the phone, saying how much she misses him, and show great delight when he arrives home. Although she is physically limited (being a hologram), she can at least supply some of the owner's emotional needs.[3]

For consumers who demand more of a physical connection, there are also sex robots. More than the stereotypical inflatable sex dolls (such as were hilariously made fun of in the 1980 movie, "Airplane!"), the newer generation sex robots also can hold a conversation. The robot, "Harmony," can make conversation and learn over time, in addition to her physical AI attributes.[4] Such sex robots were foreshadowed by Stephen Spielberg in his excellent 2001 movie, "AI Artificial Intelligence," which had a male sex robot as one of its main characters.

Another important group of lonely people is the elderly. One AARP-sponsored study concluded that one in three seniors are lonely, which creates a market opportunity for feeling AI. Trinity College Dublin has created an elder-care robot called "Stevie." In one application, at a senior citizen facility near Washington, DC, Stevie expresses sorrow about residents' illnesses, has conversations with the residents, makes comforting remarks, and even helps lead singalongs.[5]

Some applications have tried to give robots even more responsibility. At the Henn Na hotel in Japan, they put the robots almost completely in charge, including staffing the front desk with AI dinosaurs and other creatures. Unfortunately, the robots were not ready for prime time, and the hotel owners realized they had to limit the robots to tasks in which they could function effectively. They laid off about half of the robots.[6]

Although not yet as far along, some successful feeling AI applications already exist, and given the societal problem of increasing loneliness, there is a tremendous opportunity for future development.

The Changing Consumer

Use of AI changes the consumer, because many of the tasks the consumer used to do are now performed by AI. To see the implications of this, it is useful to take a historical perspective. Mechanical AI has replaced much of the consumer's physical labor. The result of this is that consumers are less physical, and pay more attention to thinking tasks and feeling tasks. In other words, the typical consumer is now more thinking-oriented than physically oriented.

As thinking AI develops, this will also have a predictable effect on the consumer. In this case, consumers will become *less* thinking-oriented, because many of the consumer's thinking tasks are now performed by AI. The result is that the consumer is increasing the emphasis on emotion, empathy, and feeling. This means that the consumer and the typical worker are evolving in the same way—away from thinking, and focusing more on soft skills and interpersonal relationships.

The increasingly feeling-oriented consumer reinforces business' shift toward feeling. Serving an emotionally driven consumer requires greater feeling intelligence on the part of the business. The Feeling Economy is one in which both business and the consumer become more emotional and empathetic. Let us consider, for example, the case of the customer service representative. The easy, repetitive tasks in serving the customer (e.g., providing information, making appointments, etc.) will be done by AI. A consumer with a nonroutine problem is much more likely to be emotionally involved, and the service person to whom AI escalates the problem will need to be much more empathetic than the traditional customer service person. The emotionality of the consumer forms a feedback loop of the following form:

> Consumer is more emotional => Business must become more emotional => which makes the consumer even more emotional => and so on.

Conclusions

The same trend toward emotionality that we are seeing in the business world also is happening with the consumer. Businesses must "dumb down" the thinking intelligence requirements for consumers, such as difficult instructions or computation. Businesses must seek, instead, to hand off thinking intelligence requirements to AI. Often the consumer interface to the business is AI-driven, which means there is a machine-to-machine connection (e.g., buying something on Amazon Prime through their website or app). This leaves the emotional connection largely to humans. To match the emotionality of the consumer, the customer-facing personnel must become more empathetic, which in turn makes the consumer even more emotionally driven.

An interesting example is a service scenario in which one of our recent doctoral graduates, an African-American man named Jared, was trying to buy a car. He started out with one salesperson, who took a more thinking-oriented approach. This was a good match for Jared, because PhDs are among the most thinking-oriented people on Earth. The salesperson, being good at his job, was trying to match Jared's interaction preferences. Unfortunately, Jared was then passed off to an African-American salesperson, no doubt to try to match Jared's cultural background and ethnicity. This salesperson, knowing that business needs to be more emotional as time goes by, tried an emotional approach with Jared, calling him "my black brother," and using other emotional appeals. Such an approach will work the vast majority of the time as consumers become more emotionally driven. For Jared, though, it was not what he needed. The one thing we know, however, is that there will be fewer and fewer thinking-oriented consumers like Jared. An emotional sales approach will usually work the best, because the consumer is increasingly emotional as AI takes over more of the thinking tasks.

Notes

1. *Statista* (2020), "Number of Smartphone Users Worldwide from 2016 to 2021," accessed at https://www.statista.com/statistics/330695/number-of-smartphone-users-worldwide/ on February 6, 2020.
2. Heisler, Steve (2019), "No Frills: Consumers Just Want the Basics from Voice Assistants," *Marketing News*, November/December, 32–39.
3. Prigg, Mark (2018), "The $1300 Holographic AI Wife That Will 'Serve Her Master' (If You Keep Paying Her $14 a Month 'Living Expenses')," *Daily Mail.com*, accessed at https://www.dailymail.co.uk/sciencetech/article-6072229/1300-holographic-AI-wife-chat-paying-14-month-living-expenses.html on February 6, 2020.
4. Keach, Sean (2019), "Creepy £7000 'Harmony' Sex-Bot with a Saucy Scottish Accent Goes on Sale—As Fear over Rise of Robot Lovers Grows," *The Sun*, accessed at https://www.thesun.co.uk/tech/8555630/harmony-sex-robot-realbotix-price/ on February 6, 2020.
5. Purtill, Corinne (2019), "Stop Me If You've Heard This One: A Robot and a Team of Irish Scientists Walk into a Senior Living Home," *Time*, accessed at https://time.com/longform/senior-care-robot/ on February 6, 2020.
6. Liao, Shannon (2019), "Japan's Robot Hotel Lays Off Half the Robots after They Created More Work for Humans," *The Verge*, accessed at https://www.theverge.com/2019/1/15/18184198/japans-robot-hotel-lay-off-work-for-humans on February 6, 2020.

11

Management in the Feeling Economy

As we move from the Thinking Economy to the Feeling Economy, management will have to change. The key to this new era is that AI will no longer be seen as subservient to humans. Instead, humans and AI will be teammates that collaborate to get work done. AI will be seen as an equal member of the team, and will increasingly assume more of the team's thinking tasks. The focus of this chapter is how best to manage this collaboration.

Management in the Feeling Economy thus requires a better understanding of the comparative strengths of human versus machine intelligences at the three intelligence levels and at different networking levels (which machines can achieve more easily than humans).

Human–Machine Collaboration—Not Machines Augmenting Humans

We adopt the concept of collaborative intelligence, which is about humans and machines complementing each other along the three AI intelligences, and leveraging AI's networking capability to make work and life better. We use the term "collaborative" to avoid the human-centric view that humans can control the intelligence level and the development path of machines, and that machines are designed to serve humans. Instead, humans and machines are seen here as equals, and hopefully, with good management, such collaboration makes each other better off. Human–machine collaboration (or complementarity) means that humans and machines each do what they are good at,

© The Author(s) 2021
R. T. Rust and M.-H. Huang, *The Feeling Economy*,
https://doi.org/10.1007/978-3-030-52977-2_11

based on the respective nature of their intelligences (i.e., how they learn and what they are good at). This is in contrast to the concept of augmentation in the Thinking Economy, which implies that machines are used to support humans (humans are superior to machines, and machines are used to "augment" humans). Collaboration does not imply human superiority; instead, it implies human–machine equality. Machines can benefit from human intelligence as well, not just serve humans. This has important implications for the management of the Feeling Economy. We discuss the comparative strengths of humans and machines below.

Human strengths. Some human intelligences are difficult for AI to mimic. (Contextual) mechanical (intuitive) thinking, and (biological) feeling intelligences are the strengths of humans.

Contextual mechanical intelligence involves eye–hand–foot coordination, finger and manual dexterities, face-to-face contact, and physical presence in a place, which are difficult for machines to perform alone.[1] The distinction between service and manufacturing captures this nuance: service provision involves contextual coproduction, whereas physical goods production does not (meaning that production and consumption are separable). This difference results in a much lower degree of service automation than manufacturing automation, due to information technology (a proxy for mechanical AI), because humans can (at this point) provide contextual service better than machines. This is what Autor and Dorn observed, the growth of low-skilled service labor and the US labor market polarization due to computerization.[2] Even if the skill level is low, when it is contextual, humans are in a better position to do it. That provided an opportunity for unskilled manufacturing workers to re-skill to become unskilled service labor in the Thinking Economy. The factory workers of the past have become the Uber drivers and DoorDash deliverers of the Thinking Economy.

Intuitive intelligence is the intuition or common sense that humans acquire or accumulate from their surroundings and interactions. It is based on real-world knowledge—a rich understanding of the world, not learned from formal education.[3] Sometimes people resort to decision shortcuts, trading accuracy for efficiency; for example, bounded rationality in behavioral economics,[4] or the peripheral route of persuasion in Petty and Cacioppo's Elaboration Likelihood Model (ELM).[5] The peripheral route is considered peripheral because when consumers see a car ad, they do not always think carefully or rationally about the cost and quality of the car, but may instead focus on the beautiful woman standing next to the car. Buying a car because of beauty does not make much sense to machines, but this kind of sex appeal is common in advertising. Machines would have difficulty behaving this way or understanding it logically. The example illustrates that intuition and common sense (along with language understanding, because understanding language requires an understanding of culture, not just grammar rules) are difficult for AI to achieve, even if they are argued to be preconditions for general intelligence.[6]

Human feeling intelligence is the ability of humans to identify one's own and others' emotions, and respond to them appropriately. It involves the ability to be aware of emotions, the ability to apply the emotions to tasks, and the ability to manage emotions.[7] Human emotion has a physiological component that is innate to biological beings, as discussed in the biological intelligences section. Emotion is a holistic experience. The chemical changes in the nervous system are associated with thinking, feeling, and behavioral responses[8]; therefore, emotion can't be separated into distinct biological components and still retain its character. Thus, the holistic experience of emotion may be the nuance that contributes most to emotional AI's failure to grasp emotions. These human abilities are difficult for machines to mimic. McDuff and Czerwinski, writing in the *Communications of the ACM*, point out that embodied agents and robots will never experience the physiological reactions nor the actual emotions that they project (for example, a racing heart or relaxation), even if research to develop machines that are seemingly emotionally sentient is advancing.[9]

Machine strengths. As AI is continually advancing, the strengths of AI discussed in this section are mostly based on the current intelligence levels of AI (mainly by neural network-based machine learning). What machines cannot do currently may not be a limitation of AI indefinitely. In terms of intelligence levels, for current machine intelligences, mechanical (analytical) thinking, and (analytical) feeling intelligences are the strengths of machines.

Machines outperforming humans at the mechanical intelligence level has a long history, as demonstrated by the various generations of the industrial revolution, that have transformed the economy from manufacturing to service by replacing low-skilled manufacturing labor and pushing those workers into the service sector. We have discussed this extensively in Chapters 2 and 3. Even in the early days before smart machines, traditional computers were considered to be smarter than humans in doing routine tasks faster and more accurately than humans.

For machine intelligences at the thinking and feeling levels, given the machine learning approach to learning, they are both data- and analytical-based. As the application of narrow AI has shown, machines can be trained to outperform humans in specific tasks, given the right data input and powerful algorithms. Depending on whether cognitive or emotional data are fed to machines, machines can be trained to demonstrate both thinking and feeling intelligences, but both in an analytical way. Such analytical-based thinking and feeling intelligences have the strengths of processing big data rapidly, which is far beyond human information processing capability.

Major Benefits of the Three Machine Intelligences

The machine strengths in mechanical tasks, in analytical thinking tasks, and in mechanical and analytical feeling tasks suggest three major benefits that machines can deliver. We have discussed these as the major economic outputs for the three economies in the previous chapters. Here we elaborate more about how they achieve these benefits:

Mechanical AI for standardization. Mechanical AI learns and adapts only to a minimal degree. It relies heavily on preinstalled algorithms and data to generate standardized outputs. The objective function is error minimization. Thus, it is ideal for standardization. We have discussed this standardization benefit in Chapter 2, the Physical Economy, driven by machinery. Even in the Feeling Economy, there are markets that mechanical AI can serve for standardization. For example, we propose a "McService" strategy in our "Technology-Driven Service Strategy" article in the *Journal of the Academy of Marketing Science*, that can be used when customers have homogeneous demand for the service, and are low in potential customer lifetime value. In that scenario, mechanical AI can be used to automate service for efficiency.[10] Examples are fast-food ordering and delivery, self-service, budget service, and customer service for routine issues. In this use of mechanical AI, routine and repetitive human service is transformed into self-service or is mass produced with standard output. For example, a smart refrigerator equipped with a sensor and camera can detect the grocery inventory level and automatically refill goods that are running short, hotel housekeeping service robots replace human employees to perform routine housekeeping service, collaborative robots (cobots) help with packaging, and drones distribute physical goods. All these applications aim to generate standardized, consistent, and reliable outcomes.

In our "Engaged to a Robot ..." paper (in the *Journal of Service Research*, we list several conditions in which mechanical AI can be used for standardization, including[11]:

- *For cost leadership.* If firms pursue a cost leadership strategy that emphasizes operational excellence, mechanical AI can be used to automate service processes to reduce costs. The more service processes can be standardized, the more process automation can be achieved by mechanical AI. For example, McDonald's uses robots to deliver ordered foods to customers, and firms use virtual bots to deliver customer service.
- *For delivery.* Mechanical AI has great potential for delivery, because delivery tasks, such as shipping, delivery, and payment, are more routine and repetitive. Use of mechanical AI can improve delivery efficiency for firms, and improve convenience for customers. We have seen many applications for these purposes already. For example, automated payment or automated delivery provides customers a smooth and uninterrupted process. Amazon's one-click buying is a classic example that allows customers to purchase with one click without having to go through the multiple steps of filling the shopping cart, providing shipping information and credit card information, etc. Being an e-commerce giant, Amazon invests heavily and experiments with various mechanical AI applications to deliver its offerings (goods and service) to customers, such as Amazon Prime Air's delivery drones.

Thinking AI for personalization. Personalization is the key benefit that thinking AI can offer. The need to personalize is based on the assumption that every customer is unique. This is very different from the mass production era assuming that consumers like to use the products that are also used by others (e.g., their neighbors, celebrities), thus making commodities appealing. The availability of big data and the analytical capability of AI make mass personalization feasible. Consumers are able to receive individualized goods and service that match their personal preferences. Such individualism was less feasible technologically in the Thinking Economy, but as AI gains in thinking capability, segmentation is becoming increasingly targeted, with the logical end being segments of size one, or personalization.

We have seen various analytical AI applications being used for this purpose, for example, Netflix's personalized movie recommendations, Amazon's personalized online shopping, online price comparison, and personalized banking, etc. Almost all businesses that have big data available can personalize accordingly. Such personalization is data-based, but it doesn't mean that only big data can be used for personalization. Small data can be used, too.

- *Big data personalization.* Personalization is not only made possible by big data. The data input in personalization can be either big data or small data.

We first discuss this in our "Technology-Driven Service Strategy" paper, and later elaborate it in our "Engaged to a Robot? ..." paper. Big data personalization involves examining many customers' data to find patterns that can then be used to provide better service to individual customers. Such an approach is viable, even if longitudinal data are not available. For example, Amazon's collaborative filtering is a big data personalization that makes use of like-minded customers' data to infer the focal customer's preferences. The personal companion depicted in the 2004 "Her" movie relies on such big data personalization. Such personalization is also ideal for identifying potential target segments. Very often machines can discover unique segments that humans fail to see, perhaps due to the rigidity of our framework of thinking.

- *Small data personalization.* Alternatively, small data personalization is only possible if there is longitudinal data. It is adaptive and dynamic.[12] Small data personalization is more challenging than big data personalization, because learning from sparse data tends to be less precise and less accurate, given current machine learning algorithms and models. The potential of small data personalization has not yet been widely recognized and should have significant managerial implications. For example, a smart personal assistant such as Alexa learns from longitudinal small data, and can better answer the consumer's questions over time. Eric Topol's experience of using an AI diet, reported in *The New York Times*, illustrates nicely the potential for small data personalization. He participated in an AI diet experiment that used a smartphone app to track the food and drink he consumed, and used a sensor to monitor his blood-glucose levels. His data, along with other consumers' data, were analyzed, and a personalized diet algorithm was created for him to help him eat healthier. The recommended diet program was fully personalized based on his data, rather than treating him as similar to other peers and recommending a generic diet, such as the Mediterranean diet.[13]

Feeling AI for relationalization. The major benefit that feeling AI can deliver is relationalization, i.e., personalized relationship. Any relationship is by definition heterogeneous across individuals. To achieve true relationalization requires true emotional machines, that is, machines that can recognize, simulate, and react to emotions appropriately (to be discussed further in Chapter 14, AI for Feeling). Here we discuss two applications, given current technologies.

- *Mechanical feeling AI for standardization.* Mechanical feeling AI, such as text-based chatbot customer service, is used to perform unskilled mechanical-like feeling tasks. These tasks, although requiring interaction and communication, can be rather standard and routine, making it possible for AI to handle, such as answering frequently asked questions on a website.
- *Analytical feeling AI for personalization.* Analytical feeling AI, such as Affectiva, uses emotional analytics (e.g., voice-mining analytics for voice-based chatbots) to personalize the interaction and communication with customers. This involves analytical AI being used to analyze small emotional data and coming up with a preferred style of communication with the consumer.

Collaboration at Different Intelligence Levels

The human strengths, machine strengths, and the benefits that different machine intelligences can deliver suggest multiple scenarios for human–machine collaboration. Table 11.1 summarizes the types of collaborative intelligence. Within each intelligence level, AI can be designed to be less intelligent, equally intelligent, or more intelligent than humans. The general principle is that it is best for lower-level AI intelligences to collaborate with higher-level human intelligence (HI), assuming the higher-level HI is the intelligence level that current AI has not achieved yet. It thus constitutes a natural boundary condition for collaborative intelligence. We discuss each of the scenarios in Table 11.1.

Table 11.1 Managing in the Feeling Economy

Stakeholder	Implications
Firms	• Think of AI and employees collaborating as a team, not AI replacing or augmenting employees
	• Recognize the power of turning private data into public data, and their implications for providing standardization, personalization, and relationalization benefits to consumers
	• Become more feeling intelligent in running the business, hiring, and interacting with consumers
Consumers	• Understand better one's own and others' emotions and emotional needs
	• Recognize the power of private data, individually or collectively, and their implications for privacy concerns
	• Re-skill, cross-skill, or up-skill feeling intelligence

Source Authors' creation

Mechanical AI + all levels of HI. Mechanical AI can work together with human contextual mechanical intelligence. For example, cobots are used as the physical extension of human field workers, such as assistants to chefs and physicians for undesirable tasks (e.g., hot soup or hot oil in the kitchen) or for better performance (i.e., precision surgeries).

Mechanical AI can collaborate with humans for better thinking. For example, in-car sensors collect driving information for the driver to drive better and for the insurance company to decide the premium.

Mechanical AI can collaborate with humans for better feeling intelligence. For example, Fitbit wearable devices collect a user's physiological data that help the user understand his/her own emotions. The AI diet example discussed earlier is another example of using a smart wearable device and sensor to collect biometric data that help the consumer eats healthier. Some consider such biotech wearables to have great potential for autistic children to understand others' emotions. Virtual reality and augmented reality are used to allow humans to have virtual experiences or make the experience more real (or better). In one example, furniture retailer IKEA uses virtual reality and augmented reality to let customers preview how furniture looks in their homes.

Analytical thinking AI + intuitive and biological feeling HI. For analytical thinking AI + intuitive HI, this type of collaboration is like using narrow AI (good at specialized tasks) to work together with general HI (good at a general job) to solve problems or make decisions. For example, the fashion clothing company Gap uses predictive analytics for fashion trends that assist human designers to design clothing to better match customer preferences. Tailor Brand's Logo Maker visualizes logo designs that help customers to self-design logos and develop branding strategies. This type of collaboration can be expected to prosper in many areas, by serving as the analytical foundation for human judgment.

For analytical thinking AI + feeling HI, such collaboration has potential for professional soft service workers (e.g., marketing managers), because thinking AI can do most of the analytical tasks, while leaving the feeling tasks to humans. For example, image-recognition AI identifies possible skin cancer cases (a strength of machine for pattern recognition) and human doctors do the feeling tasks by interacting and communicating with patients. This type of collaboration can be expected to prosper in areas such as helping humans to recognize, label, and manage emotions. The applications of thinking AI to help depression detection and treatment, and helping autistic kids to recognize and label emotions are on the way.

Analytical feeling AI + biological feeling HI. Analytical feeling AI can analyze, recognize, and simulate human interactions and emotions (text, image, audio, or video); thus, it can facilitate human EQ in many ways. For example, interactions on social media can be facilitated by emotion detection AI to know whether someone is happy or unhappy, annoyed already, bored by the conversation, etc., providing emotional analytics for a user to better assess and respond to another person's emotions. The display of emoticons in social media conversation is a manual way to show emotions, which can be done more personally or systematically by machines. In marketing, Cogito's voice analytics help call center agents identify customer moods and provide guidance for better interaction, and IBM's Watson Tone Analyzer, a sentiment analysis tool, enables chatbots to detect customer tones so that dialog strategies can be adjusted to the conversation accordingly. Affectiva provides analytical feeling AI service to various fields, such as detecting whether a driver is falling asleep while driving and issuing an alert, and helping advertisers to measure consumer emotional response to digital content, among others.

Collaboration at Different Networking Levels

Remember the two defining characteristics of AI—self-learning and networking capability? AI–HI collaboration can be achieved not only at different intelligence levels but also at different networking levels.

If we say collaborative intelligence at different intelligence levels is about how capable the AI algorithms/models are, then collaboration at different networking levels is about how valuable the data inputs are for AI to learn. Without good algorithms/models, AI is no different from traditional nonadaptive technologies. Without quality data, AI has nothing to learn.

AI can be designed to have zero, some, or full networking capability to scale up the benefits it can deliver. We discuss this type of AI–HI collaboration from the firm's use of networked AI and the consumer's use of networked AI, respectively, because the success of such collaboration largely hinges on the battle between the two sides for data value and data ownership.

The degree to which a firm should use networked AI depends on the value of public data. Public data are data that are accessible for firms to use as machine input. The alternative is private data that are only accessible by data owners (can be third-party data owners, competitors, or consumers). The more data, the more heterogeneous the data, and the more accurate the data, the higher value for AI to learn.

The degree to which a consumer should use networked AI depends on the value of private data. Private data are data that are only accessible by the consumer. The data can be individual in the consumer's personal device or account, or collective in the consumer's social network. The value of private data to the customer is the flip side of the privacy concern. When the value of private data is higher, it means that the stakes for data leakage are higher. The higher the value of the private data, the less willing the consumer is to use networked AI.

Below we discuss firm use and consumer use of varying degrees of networked AI, respectively. Figure 11.1 illustrates the decisions from both sides.

Firm's decision. If the value of public data to the firm is higher, firms will be incentivized to have machines networked to a greater degree. The conditions for valuable data can include more data available, more heterogeneous data, more accurate data, and more relevant data, etc. In all these conditions, networked AI can benefit from data. Alternatively, if most of the data are private (i.e., the amount of data available is limited), homogeneous (i.e., more data do not add value to the data), inaccurate (i.e., the data are of poor quality), or irrelevant (i.e., add no value to learning), firms may be better off designing machines to be stand-alone. As a result, depending on the value of public data, firms can design AI to have varying degrees of networking connectivity.

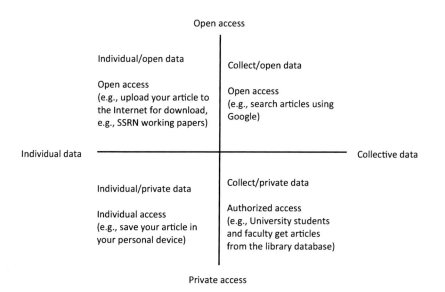

Fig. 11.1 Consumer use of AI (*Source* Authors' creation)

- *Individual AI strategy*. This is a strategy in which AI is designed to be stand-alone on both the data provider (i.e., consumer) and data receiver (i.e., firm) sides. Firms constrain their machines to have zero or limited networking capability, and consumers use such stand-alone machines in a private setting. This strategy is best when the value of public data is limited for scaling up benefits, due to most of the data being private, homogeneous, inaccurate, or irrelevant; as a result, learning from public data does not improve the benefit. Thus, an individual AI strategy should be sufficient. Additionally, this strategy can reassure consumers about their privacy. For example, Roomba claims that they don't upload consumers' floorplans to the cloud and only store those data locally in each individual machine (cleaning the consumer's house won't benefit from learning from other consumers' floor plans).
- *Individual-networked (two-sided) AI strategy*. This is a strategy that AI is networked on the firm side (back end) but is stand-alone on the consumer side. This strategy is suited to the situation when the value of public data is high, but consumers interact with AI individually in a private setting. In this scenario, firms can scale up benefits to consumers in the back end while consumers feel privacy in the front end in their interaction with their smart devices. Many personal assistants, such as Alexa, Siri, smart homes, and emotional companions, use this strategy.
- *Networked AI strategy*. This is a strategy in which AI is networked on both the firm and the consumer sides. In this strategy, AI has full networking capability, due to high public data value, and consumers interact with the AI collectively (not in a private setting). When the data value is high, this strategy can maximize the benefits of scale. For example, the Waze navigation app uses all connected drivers' input data, to provide the best route for all connected drivers.

Consumer's decision. When AI is networked, consumers can leverage the open data value but have to decide to what degree to keep their personal data private.

- *Use individual AI*. In this decision, all data are kept private. When consumers use only individual AI, it means that they prefer to keep their personal date private, sacrificing the potential scaling up benefits that they can receive. For example, wearable AI records the consumer's health data, doesn't connect to the Internet, and uses only the recorded private data to ensure the consumer's privacy while providing the service.

- *Use two-sided AI*. In this decision, only part of the data is kept private. When consumers use networked AI in their private setting, they make a distinction between public and private data. Both are valuable, but consumers want to separate them. In this consumption scenario, consumers interact with a stand-alone AI that is networked in the back end. The stand-alone consumer-facing interface ensures a private usage setting and keeps the private data local, while the networked back end allows machines to learn from public data. Personal assistant Alexa is one such example—consumers ask questions individually in a private setting and Alexa retrieves information from the Internet to answer the questions.
- *Use networked AI*. In this decision, all data are open for firms to use. When consumers use networked AI in a public setting (or use it collectively), all data are public, including consumers' private data. This means that collectively the value of data is so high that consumers are even willing to share their private data. Sharing platforms and social media data are typical examples.

Living and Working Better in the Feeling Economy

The preceding discussion illustrates types of AI–HI collaboration that can be achieved at different intelligence levels and at different networking levels. Such AI–HI collaborations can sometimes go bad. We can design machines with the goal to "augment" humans, but the self-learning path may not follow suit. We can use data in a way that follows consumers' privacy wishes, but the networking environment may not always be under control (try to think of Facebook's many data breach and leakage problems). Thus, we need to have a better understanding about how to manage these collaborations, to move the outcomes in the positive direction.

To live and work better in the Feeling Economy thus requires the Feeling Economy to develop in a positive direction for both firms and consumers, because collaboration can be achieved at all three levels of intelligences, the benefits can be magnified by AI networking capability, and both firms and consumers can use AI. A collaboration view allows a reciprocal relationship between firms and consumers (both can have machines as their agents).

To achieve so, we discuss what firms and consumers need to do for a better Feeling Economy.

Firm's management in the feeling economy. We propose that firms should (1) think of AI and employees collaborating as a team, not AI replacing or augmenting employees, (2) recognize the power of turning private data into public data, and their implications for providing standardization, personalization, and relationalizaiton benefits to consumers, and (3) become more feeling intelligent in running the business, hiring employees, and interacting with consumers.

- *AI and HI collaborate as a team.* We emphasize this repeatedly by making the distinction between collaboration and augmentation. Firms should realize that in the Feeling Economy, it is bound to be a workplace where AI and HI collaborate, rather than either AI or HI dominating individually. Therefore, firms should shift their thinking from whether AI replaces or augments employees to AI–HI collaboration.[14] Such a collaboration in the Feeling Economy means that within specific jobs, feeling tasks will become more important to human employees, leaving more of the thinking tasks to AI. It means that AI and human employees need to work as a team, based on the machine–human collaboration at the three intelligence levels outlined in the previous section. Different jobs have different task compositions. For machine–human collaboration, typically AI will assume an increasing number of the thinking tasks, and human employees will spend more of their time on feeling tasks and interactions with others.
- *Recognize the power of public data.* The boundary between private data and public data is fluid; the more valuable the private data, the stronger the motivation for the consumer to keep them private, while it also generates a stronger motivation for the firm to access the data. Thus, in managing the private–public data boundary, the firm needs to consider where to draw the line for generating the standardization benefit using mechanical AI, personalization benefit using thinking AI, and relationalization benefit using feeling AI. For example, standardization can be achieved mostly using public data, personalization can be achieved by using collective private data (e.g., adaptative personalization using the consumer' social media data), and relationalization mostly needs private emotional data, for which consumers have a greater degree of privacy concern. Moving the boundary all the way to turn all private data public is enticing for firms, but may backfire as it entails the highest degree of privacy concern.
- *Be feeling intelligent.* Firms need to focus more on the feeling and empathetic nature of business, and be more attuned to the emotional needs of employees and consumers to get (and keep) business. Just as mechanical AI automated mechanical tasks and created opportunities for thinking companies (e.g., Microsoft), thinking AI is automating more and more thinking tasks and creates new opportunities for feeling companies (e.g., Facebook).

Firms thus need to be more feeling intelligent. Furthermore, feeling intelligence may become a comparative advantage for countries with diverse populations, such as the United States, in global economic competition. Even if more authoritarian countries have a comparative advantage in the other two intelligences, they may have less capability in managing feeling intelligence. The winning strategy for the more advanced economies is to emphasize feeling intelligence, rather than going back to the Physical Economy to compete for lower cost production (we discussed in the Physical Economy chapter that China still strives to develop its manufacturing industry) or continuing to emphasize the Thinking Economy to compete with thinking AI head-to-head (e.g., India strives to develop the hard service sector, software industry).

Consumer's management in the Feeling Economy. We propose that consumers should (1) understand better one's own and others' emotions and emotional needs, (2) recognize the power of private data, individually or collectively, and their implications for privacy concerns, and (3) re-skill, cross-skill, or up-skill their feeling intelligence.

- *Understand emotional needs.* In the Feeling Economy, consumers will focus more on their feelings. Consumers, especially young consumers, are already accustomed to anywhere-anytime interaction through computers and smartphones on social media. This shift toward constant interaction results in greater reliance on feeling and social interaction for consumption decisions. For example, we have witnessed the unprecedented use of emotional shorthand, such as emoji on AI-facilitated social interactions (discussed in Chapter 5, The Age of Emoji). Those interactions seem to have different norms from other text communications. When consumers increasingly deemphasize thinking and emphasize feeling, due to the increasing use of thinking AI, and when analytical thinking AI is used to facilitate consumers' awareness of feeling and the management of it, the need to better understand self-emotions and other-emotions becomes more important.
- *Recognize the power of private data.* Private data are power. The more valuable the private data, the more power the consumer has in the economic transactions. Consumers should recognize this power of data ownership, rather than simply frame it as "privacy concerns" that convey a negative view of being afraid of losing control over data. Consumers should allow firms to use their private data, if the utility gain is greater than the privacy loss. On the contrary, consumers should deny firms to access their private

data, if the utility gain is smaller than the privacy loss. Have a profound understanding about the value of their private data (and the utility gain from those data), and the costs associated with a more open access of those data can help consumers to gain control over their own data.

- *Skill for feeling intelligence.* As AI becomes more capable of thinking, consumers need to re-skill, cross-skill, or up-skill their feeling intelligence. We have discussed these skilling requirements for employment in Chapter 4 for employees (see Table 4.2). Those can be applied to consumers, too. In the Feeling Economy, consumers also need to improve their feeling intelligence, by re-skilling (if they are very unskilled with respect to people skills and social skills to begin with), up-skilling (to improve their people and social skills), or cross-skilling (if they are the thinking type by nature). We have seen too many instances in social media in which some consumers do not have good people and social skills (e.g., cyberbullying, cruel Twitter tweets) that hurt other consumers, intentionally or unintentionally.

Firm–Consumer Interactions Change, Too

Firms and consumers do not use AI totally independently. Their interactions will change too, and that has implications for how best to cope with the Feeling Economy. We discuss some important implications of these changes at the three intelligence levels and at the networking levels.

Blame mechanical AI? When both firms and consumers can each use AI as their agents for economic transactions, the traditional trust and liability mechanisms may not apply for such machine-to-machine interactions. For example, when consumers use virtual reality or augmented reality for a more immersive digital experience to buy a piece of furniture from IKEA, they are interacting with those machines fully or partially, not with human employees. Both sides need to be aware of this longer and more complex chain of inter- actions and better prepared about how to achieve a win-win. If the consumers are not happy with the furniture they purchase via virtual reality, should IKEA be held accountable for a full refund? Andy Parker, the father of a journalist, Alison Parker, who was brutally murdered, and whose murder was widespread on YouTube, tried to get Google (the parent company of YouTube) to remove the footage, but Google replied that he can flag the footage once he found it, and then they will remove it. The problem is that Google uses AI to automatically upload videos to YouTube, but the father can only do such checks manually, making it virtually impossible to detect all the footages that are shared on YouTube. He asked Google to do this automatically, and questioned whether Google actually has humans doing such content checks for uploaded videos. Google replied that it has 10,000 people doing that, not just machines, but that is doubted. This story shows the asymmetrical power between the firm and the consumer. The firm is in a better position to use AI as its agent whereas the consumer may not have the same ability to do so.

Get stereotyped by thinking AI? There are bias, discrimination, and aversion associated with AI and its applications. John Giannandrea, Google's AI leader, urges to pay attention to AI biases, such as AI's learning human prejudices.[15] Even in cases where a technology is designed for a particular purpose, it is difficult to foresee whether and to what degree it will be used for this purpose. In 2019, Sahil Chinoy, a graphics editor for *The New York Times* Opinion section, asks the question, "are we more likely to be criminals because we look like criminals?" when he observes that the US Immigration and Customers Enforcement uses facial recognition on driver's license photographs, and criticizes that recognizing emotions based on facial expressions runs the risk of biological determinism such that we are "how we are" because of our genetic makeup, such as race and sex.[16] We have pointed out in Chapter 9 that managers and management education currently underprepare the next generation for feeling and emotional intelligence. As machine learning is not neutral, firms and consumers need to have a better understanding about how machines learn, and the differences between machine intelligence and human intelligence. Firms need to develop strategies to alleviate AI biases, and consumers need to understand the biases and better cope with the biases inherent machine learning.

Become lonelier with feeling AI? With the emergence of the Feeling Economy, many firms are tending to consumers' emotional needs, and use AI for this purpose (mostly using mechanical feeling AI or analytical feeling AI). Some consumers obtain emotional comfort from firms attending to their emotional needs, while some consumers become even more withdrawn from human interaction, since machines are sufficient for such a purpose. This is an issue of managing human attachments toward an AI system.

Will the use of more feeling AI result in more withdrawal from human interaction? Older Americans are becoming lonelier, but using robot home companions may make some consumers feel even lonelier or even more withdrawn from real-world social interactions. Instead of interacting with humans, now more and more consumers are interacting with machines. During the coronavirus outbreak, the need for social distancing forces us to rely on machines to a much greater extent for social interactions. Many of us feel lonelier and more isolated, rather than comforted. This experience shows that machines cannot totally replace human social interactions. Both firms and consumers need to find a balance between machine and human interactions.

Turn off personalization? Consumers should be able to turn off personalization when their privacy concerns are high. In this situation, they keep their data private. The more consumers keep their data private, the less open data that firms can use to scale up benefits. Thus, firms and consumers should act to encourage a virtuous cycle for data sharing and usage, rather than a vicious cycle that will eventually result in firms having no data to use and consumers receiving limited benefit from firms. We further illustrate how a consumer can manage the degree of accessibility of their private data, using the example of accessing original online content.

Consumers can keep data in their own private device, in an account, or in the cloud, allowing varying degrees of accessibility. *Data in device* have the lowest degree of accessibility (searchability); they are individual/private data that only the device owner can access to it (e.g., store your article in your smartphone). *Data in account* have limited accessibility; only authorized individuals can access it (e.g., university students and faculty can get your article from the university library database). *Data in cloud* have open access; anyone can use Google (or other search engines) to search for your article. Using how a consumer can access an article as an illustrative example below, assuming the consumer produces creative content, in this case an article:

- Individual data allowing only private access: The consumer keeps the article in his/her personal computer without sharing with anyone. This is the lowest degree of data access that only allows personal access. The article is not searchable on the Internet. The consumer is likely to do this when the paper is still work-in-progress.
- Individual data allowing open access: The consumer uploads the article to the Internet as a working paper that allows all other consumers to download. We can see many authors do this for an early and quick distribution of their papers.
- Collective data allowing only private access: Articles can be accessed by the consumer via university library authorization, if the consumer is affiliated with the university.
- Collective data allowing open access: Articles can be accessed by the consumer via an open search on Google.

Conclusions

This chapter summarizes the principal ways in which firms and consumers will need to change and manage to live and work better in the Feeling Economy, as AI assumes more thinking tasks, and employees become more focused on feeling tasks. Increasingly, both managers and consumers will collaborate with AI on a more equal basis. Typically, AI will support "higher" levels of human intelligence that AI cannot easily match. Control of the data that enables AI is crucial. As they gain access to their own AI, consumers will begin to even up the power imbalance. This suggests that companies will be wise to adopt a more enlightened view of customer data, using customer wishes to guide the degree to which data are networked.

Notes

1. Frey, Carl Benedikt, and Michael A. Osborne (2017), "The Future of Employment: How Susceptible Are Jobs to Computerisation?" *Technological Forecasting and Social Change*, 114 (January), 254–280.
2. Autor, David H., and David Dorn (2013), "The Growth of Low-Skill Service Jobs and the Polarization of the US Labor Market," *American Economic Review*, 103 (5), 1553–1597.
3. Davis, Ernest, and Gary Marcus (2015), "Commonsense Reasoning and Commonsense Knowledge in Artificial Intelligence," *Communications of the ACM*, 58 (9), 93–103.
4. Thaler, R. H. (1985), "Mental Accounting and Consumer Choice," *Marketing Science*, 4 (3), 199–214.
5. Petty, R. E., and Cacioppo, J. T. (1986), *Communication and Persuasion: Central and Peripheral Routes to Attitude Change*, New York: Springer-Verlag.
6. Schoenick, Carissa, Peter Clark, Oyvind Tafjord, Peter Turney, and Oren Etzioni (2017), "Moving Beyond the Turing Test with the Allen AI Science," *Communications of the ACM*, 60 (9), 60–64.
7. Emotional Intelligence (2019), *Psychology Today* (September 14), https://www.psychologytoday.com/intl/basics/emotional-intelligence.
8. Panksepp, Jaak (2005), *Affective Neuroscience: The Foundations of Human and Animal Emotions*, Oxford: Oxford University Press.
9. McDuff, Daniel, and Mary Czerwinski (2018), "Designing Emotionally Sentient Agents," *Communications of the ACM*, 61 (12), 74–83.
10. Huang, Ming-Hui, and Roland T. Rust (2017), "Technology-Driven Service Strategy," *Journal of the Academy of Marketing Science*, 45 (6), 906–924.
11. Huang, Ming-Hui, and Roland T. Rust (2020), "Engaged to a Robot? The Role of AI in Service," *Journal of Service Research*, Online First.

12. Chung, Tuck Siong, Michel Wedel, and Roland T. Rust (2016), "Adaptive Personalization Using Social Networks," *Journal of the Academy of Marketing Science*, 44 (1), 66–87.
13. Topol, Eric (2020), "The A.I. Diet," *The New York Times*, Artificial Intelligence Issue, 46–49.
14. Rouse, William B., and James C. Spohrer (2020), "Automating Versus Augmenting Intelligence," *Journal of Enterprise Transformation*, forthcoming.
15. Knight, Will (2017), "Forget Killer Robots-Bias Is the Real AI Danger," *MIT Technology Review* (October 3), https://www.technologyreview.com/s/608986/forget-killer-robotsbias-is-the-real-ai-danger/.
16. Chinoy, Sahil (2019), "The Racist History Behind Facial Recognition," *The New York Times*, Artificial Intelligence Issue, 34–37.

12

Moral, Ethical, and Governance Implications

As the Feeling Economy emerges, there are likely to be quite a few new issues that will arise, that will challenge us morally and ethically, and will create new demands with respect to governance. Although the Feeling Economy will create new opportunities, it will also cause serious job dislocations. Related to this is the threat of increasing income and wealth inequality. The rise of Thinking AI may also result in unintended consequences that arise from our imperfect understanding of how to manage AI. One such consequence is the possibility of bias and discrimination resulting even from totally rational algorithms. Also under threat will be our privacy.

New technologies are almost always used for war, also, which is likely to form the basis for a new arms race. There is also the possibility that AI can go rogue, in ways unanticipated. There is also the concern that AI may cause harm, leading to the issue of how to manage the liability arising from damages arising from the use of AI. Finally, there is the possibility of "robot rights," which is likely to become an issue as AI becomes more intelligent.

Job Loss

In previous chapters we have discussed the likelihood of job loss resulting from AI assuming an increasing number of thinking tasks. Although any new economy also produces new opportunities, as we saw when the Physical Economy gave way to the Thinking Economy, there is also the problem that many jobs are either lost or profoundly transformed. Thus, as the Thinking Economy emerged, the Physical Economy jobs declined, resulting

© The Author(s) 2021
R. T. Rust and M.-H. Huang, *The Feeling Economy*,
https://doi.org/10.1007/978-3-030-52977-2_12

in fewer farmers, miners, and factory workers. Likewise, the Feeling Economy will threaten many Thinking Economy jobs. For example, iHeartMedia, a company that owns more than 850 radio stations in the United States, announced recently that it would fire hundreds of workers, largely to create "AI-enabled Centers of Excellence," that would enable them to modernize, making "significant investments…in technology and artificial intelligence."[1]

The issue is how to deal with this job loss in a humane way that helps workers avoid becoming obsolete. One way, as we discussed in Chapter 9, is retraining. In particular, Thinking Economy workers must be retrained to develop their skills related to emotional intelligence, empathy, communication, and interpersonal relationships. Just as many Physical Economy workers floundered when faced with the emerging Thinking Economy, we cannot assume that Thinking Economy workers will find it easy and natural to develop the necessary new skills. This suggests that the government may need to play an important role in getting people back on their feet.

There are precedents that can inspire what is needed now. For example, when the American soldiers came home from World War II, the federal government offered a GI Bill, which offered educational opportunities for those who had served. This became a springboard to the middle class for many low-income people. Today, a similar plan can help the Thinking Economy workers to learn the skills necessary to compete in the Feeling Economy. Such a program requires a very significant investment, but the alternative is a large group of obsolete workers and social unrest.

Wealth Inequality

It is perhaps not widely understood that the advance of Thinking AI that is ushering in the Feeling Economy also inevitably results in greater inequality of wealth. In his book, *The Fourth Industrial Revolution*, Klaus Schwab notes that AI is enabling companies to make more money with fewer workers, and laborers are receiving lower wages.[2] The reason for this is that when AI performs tasks of value to society, the profits go to capital and not labor. In other words, instead of 1000 workers building a car, there might be a handful of technologists who are managing the AI that builds the cars. The result is that more of the profit goes to the owners of the machines (the capitalists) rather than the workers. The French economist, Thomas Piketty, in his book, *Capital in the Twenty-First Century*, lists many negatives associated with too much profit going to capital rather than labor. For our purposes, the key realization is that AI's benefits will go mostly to the owners (the capitalists) rather than the workers.

If an increasing percentage of the profits goes to the owners, then a large number of workers who may have previously earned attractive wages, are left out. We have seen one generation of this kind of dislocation already, as the Thinking Economy automated the factories and farms. When mass unemployment resulted, governments responded by building a stronger social safety net. In the United States, Franklin Roosevelt's New Deal created many job-creating federal agencies, and also the Social Security system.

One solution to this problem, suggested by Richard Freeman, is to expand ownership from the few to the many.[3] In other words, the capitalists should share more of their earnings with the workers. The problem with this solution is that capitalists are highly unlikely to agree to such an arrangement. So, unless the government can mandate division of earnings, this plan is not likely to succeed.

As the Feeling Economy emerges, a similar approach may be necessary, to help those who have been left behind. One idea that is now being proposed is the Universal Basic Income. In that plan, everybody in the country gets a guaranteed minimum income, which can keep people able to afford food and housing. There are concerns about whether such a program creates a moral hazard (i.e., why work if you can get paid to sit at home?), but without such a program, the risk of social unrest may increase to an intolerable extent.

Mathematician Bruce Boghosian has shown, theoretically and empirically, that only redistribution of wealth stops societies from becoming oligarchies in which a few people own the lion's share of the wealth. He shows, using a casino metaphor, that the rich will tend to get richer and the poor poorer, unless there is a mechanism of redistribution.[4] In many advanced economies there is such a redistributive mechanism (a progressive tax structure). In countries that fail to have such a mechanism (e.g., Russia after the fall of the Soviet Union), oligarchs emerge. It may be the case that AI, which otherwise will accelerate income inequality, will need to be counterbalanced by an increased wealth redistribution effort.

Human Atrophy

If humans don't exercise their capabilities, those capabilities atrophy. For example, in the Physical Economy, many workers were physically fit, because they worked hard physically all day long, mining coal, working in a factory, or plowing a field. As the Thinking Economy emerged, more of the physical work was done by machines—in the United States this has resulted in a population that is more obese than ever before, with many of the physical problems related to obesity, such as diabetes, heart trouble, and high blood pressure.

Today, as the Feeling Economy emerges, it is the thinking "muscles" that are atrophying. With people less able to think critically, there are some important consequences. For example, a democracy can only function effectively if the population is well-informed and can process information. Both of those things are currently in decline. As we discussed in Chapter 8, the result is that charisma and emotion now "trump" intelligence and reason. This problem is exacerbated in the United States by the fact that the less educated (and less wealthy) states now dominate the Senate. The solution to this problem is far from obvious. It may be, for example, that a purely democratic system no longer works. An attractive alternative to democracy is hard to think of, however. It seems as though at least a minimal degree of thinking skill should still be required educationally, if only to keep the political system operating smoothly. Perhaps the educational system could emphasize a few basic thinking skills that are relevant to civic participation, such as (1) knowledge of how the government works, (2) learning how to evaluate the validity of an argument, and (3) learning how to evaluate the credibility of an information source.

Unintended Consequences

So far, AI will do what we program it to do. That will not always be the case, as we argue in Chapter 15. But, even if we think we can control AI, we may sometimes be mistaken. Consider the example of a Thinking AI system that is taught to eliminate cancer. That sounds great until we realize that AI might find that the most efficient route to that goal is simply to kill every human on Earth.[5]

One might counter that we would never be so stupid as to program AI in that way. But increasingly Thinking AI is hard for humans to understand. For example, deep learning neural networks are essentially a black box. Human chess players studying AI games find that they often cannot find intuitive reasons for AI's moves. As AI develops further, the way machines think is likely to continue to diverge from how humans think. This will make it much more difficult to understand what AI is doing, and why it is doing it. As

AI becomes more opaque, the danger of unintended consequences increases significantly.

Bias from AI

AI also increases the threat of discrimination and bias. Sometimes the bias arises from the programmer unwittingly transmitting his/her own personal biases onto the machine. Even if this concern is avoided, however, the problem is not solved. A recent example of this was Apple Card. The company uses an AI algorithm to set credit limits. They were recently embarrassed by examples of what appear to be overt discrimination. Ironically, Apple co-founder, Steve Wozniak, was a victim of this. He and his wife applied for Apple Cards and even though Woz and his wife share their finances, live in the same household, and have the same income, Steve was offered a credit limit several times larger than his wife's. It certainly seems as though the company's algorithm was discriminating against Ms. Wozniak because she was a woman.

Such discrimination is not even good business. As Kalinda Ukanwa, a former University of Maryland doctoral student now on the faculty of the University of Southern California, showed in her dissertation, even if there is a short-term benefit to discriminating, in the long run, under commonly found conditions, discrimination is less profitable. She concludes that a "group blind" approach (not using information about such things as gender or race) is called for in such a circumstance.[6]

Even if a group-blind policy is employed, that still may not be enough. The reason is that there may be observed variables that correlate with protected groups. For example, in the United States, African-Americans may on average have a lower income, a lower educational level, and live in a segregated neighborhood (none of that is actually true of Kalinda, who is African-American). In such a case, discrimination based on income, education, or neighborhood may result in seeming discrimination against African-Americans. The key test for discrimination is whether two people who have identical characteristics, with the exception of group membership, are still treated equally. We see from this that simple statistics, such as the percentage of baseball managers who are African-Americans, may not necessarily be sufficient to establish discrimination. How to protect specific groups from discrimination using AI is an ongoing topic of research, and at this point the problem is not solved satisfactorily.

It is possible that AI will even reduce bias. The idea is that if there are robots in the workforce, then the differences between the AI workers and the human workers are likely to exceed the differences between the human workers. This "frames" the comparison, such that the human differences now appear smaller. Therefore, there might not be as much discrimination against humans (there might, however, potentially be significant discrimination against AI!).[7] It is not clear whether this effect would still hold if the AI workers are not humanoid.

Privacy Concerns

AI in business usually does its work using consumer "big data." The more data AI has, the better it can do its work. This has resulted in marketers using AI on an increasing amount of data, for the purpose of better personalization. Better personalization is a win-win, since customers prefer personalized service. The problem is that there is a trade-off between privacy and personalization. The two extremes are well-represented by a pair of quotes. Science fiction writer Isaac Asimov (the same person who devised the famous "three laws of robotics") said, "The advance of civilization is nothing but an exercise in the limiting of privacy," and libertarian author Ayn Rand said, "Civilization is the progress toward a society of privacy." Rust's own research, with P. K. Kannan and Na Peng, supports Asimov's position. Without government intervention, the advance of technology will cause privacy to diminish.[8] This means that the importance of privacy is certain to increase, and methods that enable personalization with the least sacrifice of privacy should be an active area of research.[9]

Killer AI

AI is increasingly used for warfare.[10] It can help missiles or drones find a target, and can kill without direct human intervention. In 2019, an armada of flying drones and cruise missiles, seemingly at the direction of Iran or groups supporting Iran, penetrated Saudi Arabian airspace for a devastating attack on the Saudi oil facilities. The attack was incredibly precise—much more precise than would have been possible with human guidance alone.

The use of AI as a killing machine creates unsettling moral dilemmas. Automatic action and response is certainly fast, but may result in unintended consequences. For example, in 1983 the Soviet Union experienced a false alarm in which their automated systems showed that there was an incoming nuclear missile. Fortunately, in that case, a human intervened and refused to launch a counterattack. Almost four decades later, it is easy to imagine such a system being totally automated and run by AI. That might land us in World War III, without any human having made the conscious decision.

Former US Secretary of State, Henry Kissinger, joined with Google/Alphabet's Eric Schmidt and MIT's Daniel Huttenlocher to consider what AI means for international defense and security. They conclude that the unexplainability aspect of AI may be problematic in this scenario. If one side can't figure out the other side's decision making, then threatening interactions become more unpredictable. In some cases, a competitor may decide that a preemptive strike is the least risky strategy.[11]

Liability Concerns

There is always the possibility that AI will go wrong, and someone will be harmed. For example, there was an accident in which a Tesla, running on autopilot, crashed into a truck, killing the Tesla's driver. Several such accidents have been reported since 2016. In 2018, an Uber self-driving car ran over a woman who was crossing the street.

The nature of liability in such a situation is not particularly clear. Who takes liability for accidental harm? Is it the human user, the manufacturer, or the AI entity itself? It seems unfair to blame the human user for something AI does wrong, but on the other hand, it was apparently the user who chose to use AI in the first place. This may be analogous to gun liability. If a person shoots someone, we typically blame the shooter and not the gun. Analogous reasoning would conclude that it is the human using the AI who should be liable.

On the other hand, if AI is created in such a way that it is unsafe, that would seem to be the manufacturer's fault. The legal field of product liability tends to hold the manufacturer responsible if they should have reasonably known that their product was dangerous. One problem with this is that many forms of modern AI (e.g., deep learning neural nets) are essentially black boxes, in that much of their decision making cannot be easily explained. In other words, the AI may be dangerous, and yet the manufacturer does not know it. In such a case, the product needs to be in the field before we find out whether it is dangerous or not. In such a case, it is not clear whether the manufacturer should still assume liability.

Eventually, as AI becomes intelligent enough to rival human intelligence, it may be reasonable to begin thinking of AI in a different way. As we have seen foreshadowed in many science fiction movies (e.g., "Blade Runner," "Her") a deep and nuanced intelligence may provoke humans to have strong emotional reactions. We may begin to think of AI, especially anthropomorphic AI robots, as being more like people. At that point, maybe it makes sense for the AI to assume liability itself.

Robot Rights

Already, there is a robot citizen. Sophia, a robot created by Hanson Robotics, was named a citizen of Saudi Arabia in 2017. Although that seemed to be mostly a publicity stunt, it raised important issues about how to treat our intelligent AI entities, and whether robots, like people, should have essential rights. Here is a sampling of the moral and governance issues that arise from AI that approaches human intelligence:

- At what level of intelligence do we say that an AI entity is worthy of protection?
- If we turn off an intelligent AI entity, is that murder?
- If the AI is re-programmed, is it the same AI?
- If AI does something wrong, is it guilty, and should it be punished (or destroyed)?
- Should AI own property?
- Should AI vote?
- Should AI run for office?
- Should discrimination against AI entities be illegal?

Kissinger et al. recommend that a new field of AI ethics be created, to explore the ethics of administering AI. It seems reasonable to extend the scope of the field to include the ethics of the AI entity itself.

Conclusions

As AI becomes more advanced, and develops better thinking intelligence, the Feeling Economy will be faced with several important issues with respect to moral, ethical, and governance. Many people in Thinking Economy jobs will be displaced, leading to a societal imperative for retraining, so that the displaced workers are not permanently lost. Because more work will be done by AI (which is typically owned by capitalists) rather than workers, more of the wealth of AI will be gathered by the capitalists rather than the workers, potentially leading to extreme inequality of income and wealth. Strong efforts of wealth redistribution may be required to counteract the concentration of wealth. At the same time, AI's dominance in thinking tasks may dumb down the human population (in terms of thinking intelligence). This may have worrisome implications for informed voting and civic engagement. Other potential negatives include biased algorithmic decision making and loss of privacy.

As AI increases in capability, we need to start thinking about it differently. At a sufficiently high intelligence level, AI is more like a human than a pocket calculator. This creates profound issues with respect to autonomous war fighting, liability, and eventually "robot rights." Eventually, AI seems likely to be more like our peer than our servant, which raises some thorny moral issues.

Notes

1. Harwell, Drew (2020), "U.S. Radio's Top Player Blames AI for Layoffs—DJs Say That's Spin," *Washington Post*, February 9, G1.
2. Schwab, Klaus (2016), *The Fourth Industrial Revolution*, New York: Crown Business.
3. Freeman, Richard B. (2018), "Ownership When AI Robots Do More of the Work and Earn More of the Income," *Journal of Participation and Employee Ownership*, 1 (1), 74–95.
4. Boghosian, Bruce M. (2019), "The Inescapable Casino," *Scientific American*, November, 70–77.
5. Reid, Corinne (2020), "Artificial Intelligence Will Do What We Ask—That's a Problem," *Quanta Magazine*, accessed at https://www.quantamagazine.org/artificial-intelligence-will-do-what-we-ask-thats-a-problem-20200130/ on April 21, 2020.
6. Ukanwa, Kalinda, and Roland T. Rust (2020), "Algorithmic Discrimination in Service," University of Maryland working paper.
7. Jackson, Joshua Conrad, Noah Castelo, and Kurt Gray (2020), "Could a Rising Robot Workforce Make Humans Less Prejudiced," *American Psychologist*, accessed at https://psycnet.apa.org/record/2020-00794-001 on April 21, 2020.
8. Rust, Roland T., P.K. Kannan, and Na Peng (2002), "The Customer Economics of Internet Privacy," *Journal of the Academy of Marketing Science*, 30 (4), 455–464.

9. Schneider, Matthew J., Sharan Jagpal, Sachin Gupta, and Yan Yu (2017), "Protecting Customer Privacy when Marketing with Second-Party Data," *International Journal of Research in Marketing*, 34 (3), 593–603.
10. Sharkey, Noel (2020), "Autonomous Warfare," *Scientific American*, February, 52–57.
11. Kissinger, Henry A., Eric Schmidt, and Daniel Huttenlocher (2019), "The Metamorphosis," *The Atlantic*, August, 24–26.

13

Artificial Creativity

Can AI really be creative? Creativity has long been considered a capability unique to humans. We discussed in the previous chapters that thinking AI is currently mainly at the analytical level. Although research on intuitive AI is progressing, this intelligence level represents a bottleneck for computer scientists. Nevertheless, we are seeing more and more music and art created by machines. Are they creative? Do you like them? Is the question of whether something is creative decided by machines or humans? In 2018, *Bloomberg Businessweek* featured AI-generated paintings by Robbie Barrat, a Stanford researcher, who fed thousands of example paintings to machines for them to learn about how to create paintings.[1] The cover page painting looks like an artwork of impressionism. Does this show that machines can be creative? We try to answer this question in this chapter.

How Do Machines Learn?

In discussing the Physical Economy, we viewed thinking AI as just one overall AI intelligence. Later, in discussing the Thinking Economy, we borrowed our original conceptualization, in the 2018 *Journal of Service Research* paper "Artificial Intelligence in Service," in which we laid out four AI intelligences, from mechanical, to analytical, to intuitive, to empathetic.[2] The distinction between analytical intelligence and intuitive intelligence at the thinking level is important for answering the question of whether AI can be creative, and how AI can be creative, because intuitive intelligence is the backbone technology of artificial creativity (feeling intelligence is also important for art).

© The Author(s) 2021
R. T. Rust and M.-H. Huang, *The Feeling Economy*,
https://doi.org/10.1007/978-3-030-52977-2_13

Intuitive intelligence is an intermediate step between thinking and feeling, because it extends machine thinking from rational to bounded rational, to allow intuition and commonsense reasoning.

The two levels of thinking intelligence coincide with two distinct approaches in the way that machines learn. Although modern AI mainly acquires intelligence through mapping (i.e., machine learning), mapping is not the only approach to AI. We discuss this briefly in Chapter 3, the Thinking Economy. Here we elaborate the two approaches to learning, to provide a technological foundation about whether machines can be creative, to what degree machines can be creative, and how machines can be creative. Figure 13.1 illustrates the two approaches to learning. There are numerous algorithms and their combinations that can be used in both approaches. We only list some for illustrative purpose.

Mapping approach. The current approach to AI is a mapping mechanism that views machines as narrow AI to perform specific tasks. Basically, machines learn from mapping input pairs (X, Y) to output Y = F(X). One trains a machine (i.e., a neural network, or many layers of networks in the case of deep learning) with the (X, Y) pairs. If X, then Y, and if not Y, then not X. This is called training. After the training, the machine can predict Y when it is given a new X.[3] X can be any data, text, audio, or video, and the mapping is achieved by algorithms. Although this sounds like a dumb approach, if combined with super computing power, this is the approach that has given rise to the current AI "Spring," because it can map whatever types of data (typically big, unstructured) to outcomes. A layman may not be aware that the so-called smart machines learn in this very simple and straightforward way. This is an application of the analytical level of thinking intelligence that we talk about.

This data mapping approach to learning does not require machines to have domain knowledge, to have a deep understanding of questions or environments, to answer questions. Consequently, we cannot easily explain "why" a

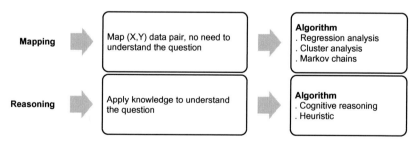

Fig. 13.1 Mapping and reasoning approaches to learning (*Source* Authors' creation)

machine generates Y. For example, Lewis and Denning illustrate that Netflix's recommender network has a customer's entire film viewing history, his/her ratings, and other customers' ratings as the X, and has recommendation of a new film as Y that the customer is likely to enjoy watching. We know that the likelihood for this customer to watch film Y is higher than non-Y, but we don't know why the customer likes Y. This gives rise to the "explainable AI" issue that we will discuss later.

Reasoning approach. This approach to machine intelligence designs machines to have strong AI (or general AI) that is expected to be able to handle all kinds of tasks, just as humans have multiple intelligences to solve general problems. Computer scientists started from this approach to developing machines. It was called expert systems or knowledge management systems, such that machines accumulate their knowledge (like humans learn from education to become more knowledgeable and skilled with more school year education) to solve problems. This approach is intuitive, in that it develops machines to think like humans. Unfortunately, given the "bytes" (0 and 1) nature of computing, programing machines to be able to do cognitive reasoning (by applying knowledge) is too complicated and infeasible without super computing power. This has resulted in several AI "Winters" in which many people gave up on developing cognitive machines. Successful application of the reasoning approach requires the intuitive level of thinking intelligence. In human learning language, we call this kind of reasoning approach as "understanding" the question and figuring out the answer.

With new and diverse approaches to AI continuing to evolve for machines to mimic higher levels of human intelligence, and with the continuing increase of computing power and decrease of computing costs, the scope of AI is moving closer to the multiple human capabilities that machines may not have now. For example, SingularityNET established a decentralized global AI network aiming to foster the development of general AI by assembling complementary narrow AI agents together. Microsoft recently announced that it will partner with OpenAI to develop general AI. *CNN* business writer Clare Duffy reports that IBM announced recently that its AI system, Watson, had a breakthrough in becoming more fluent in human debate. This Project Debater advances the natural language processing capability of Watson to be able to identify and make sense of colloquialisms and idioms. For example, it can understand that "open a can of worms" does not mean someone is actually opening a can of worms.[4]

Can Data Mapping Be Creative?

Since we don't have intuitive machines yet, can data mapping be creative? We illustrate two real-world examples to explore the answer.

Englishman Ed Newton-Rex was a music major who became interested in AI. He created a musical composition system called Jukedeck, that has written more than a million songs.[5] The brains behind Jukedeck (besides the inventor's) was a deep learning neural network approach that analyzed thousands of existing songs. This caused the algorithm to "learn" what made a song successful, and then use that information to create new songs. Similar start-ups have emerged worldwide, causing concern in the music industry that songwriters might soon be out of business.

In 2018, Lexus launched a "Driven by Intuition" TV commercial with the script totally created by IBM Watson, a cognitive technology striving to have intuitive intelligence based on machine learning. Creating a product-selling commercial is considered to require creativity. Those positions in an advertising agency are even called creative executives or creative managers, indicating the central role of creativity in designing ads.

The script of the 60-second commercial was written by applying the machine learning approach. Lexus fed machines with 15 years of award-winning luxury ads, Lexus brand data, and emotion data, that were shown to connect with viewers, to tell the story about how Lexus generated the new ES executive saloon car. All these data are X, which have all components that a successful ad should have. Machines then generate Y, the script. The commercial appears to have face validity as a luxury car commercial. However, can this commercial sell Lexus car or only generate buzz? We apply some strategic marketing considerations to analyze this commercial, and conclude that the ad is ambiguous about what it wants to achieve. It has an unclear customer segmentation and ambiguous value proposition (positioning). It appears to be a combination of various pieces of luxury car commercials. Although the ad was novel and generated wide discussion, whether it could be considered as an effective commercial for selling Lexus car is a question mark.

What does this example say? Machines are good at identifying pieces (e.g., the ingredients of a commercial) and putting these pieces together, but whether these pieces together constitute a meaningful whole is another question. Does this qualify as "creativity?" When we say that the commercial may not meet strategic marketing considerations, it also begs the question of who is in the position to evaluate whether the commercial is creative or not. We discuss this issue in the next section.

What Is Artificial Creativity?

To answer this question, we need to address two issues: what is creativity and who evaluates the creativity? It is typically considered that creativity is about something new. This simple definition does not reveal the whole story of creativity. For example, how new is new enough to be considered as creative, and if the new idea is disliked, is it still creative? We see from history that time horizon also plays a role. A piece of work may be disliked at the time when it is invented, but become liked at a much later time (very often after the death of the artist). For example, Vincent van Gogh, one of the greatest artists of all time, was largely unknown in his lifetime, although all of his paintings are worth millions of dollars today.

How new is new? How new is new is about the way and the degree new ideas are different from the existing ones. Margaret Boden, in her 1998 *Artificial Intelligence* article, "Creativity and Artificial Intelligence," discussed three types of creativity: (1) combinational creativity (novel combinations of familiar ideas), (2) exploratory creativity (new ideas in an existing conceptual space), and (3) transformational creativity (new ideas in a new conceptual space).[6]

Combinational creativity is the lowest level of creativity, in which new ideas are generated by combining familiar ideas. For example, consider a new rock 'n' roll song, perhaps incorporating stylistic elements from other genres. Although it is a new song, and has some new characteristics, listeners can easily tell it is rock 'n' roll. Thus, for example, when Johnny Cash included Mexican instrumentation in his song, "Ring of Fire" (based on a dream, according to accounts), there was still no mistaking the song's country heritage (the song was written by his wife, June Carter Cash, who grew up in the legendary Carter family, one of the most influential early country groups).

Exploratory creativity is more novel than the combinational version. New ideas are generated in an existing conceptual space. For example, songwriter Bob Dylan merged Woody Guthrie protest songs with rock & roll, creating a new form that had both rhythmic drive and complexity of lyrics. His music was hugely influential on the greatest musicians of the 1960s, including Jimi Hendrix and the Beatles. He ultimately was awarded the Nobel Prize for literature.

Transformational creativity is the highest level of creativity, in which new ideas are generated as a new conceptual space. For example, the German band Kraftwerk showed up on stage in the 1970s with only synthesizers and drum machines, some of which they invented themselves.[7] This was a total break with the past, involving both new instrumentation and a new song type that evolved into modern electronica (and even hip hop).

Currently machines can easily achieve combinational creativity using machine learning.[8,9] The opening quote from *Bloomberg Businessweek* about the AI-generated impressionist style painting is such an example. By feeding machines with tones of impressionist painting, the machines are able to combine ideas in these existing paintings into a new painting. AI has also been used to create sets of electronic dance music.[10] The Lexus car commercial falls into this category too. A new commercial is generated by extracting data from the past 15 years' award-winning ads, along with other types of data. Now, the question is, by feeding a machine with tons of impressionist paintings, can machines generate new paintings at the exploratory and transformational levels? This means that the new painting should not just be a mix of existing impressionist paintings, but should be a new style of impressionist paintings (e.g., post-impressionism as exploratory creativity) or even a new style such as expressionist, to be qualified as transformational creativity. If we feed machines with various styles of paintings, then they may be able to generate some exploratory-level paintings because the boundary of conceptual space is blurred (or expanded). This turns us to the next issue: who is to evaluate which level of creativity a machine output has achieved?

Who evaluates creativity? The second issue about creativity is who evaluates the new ideas, that is, whose perspective and taste count? Novel ideas are not equal to creative ideas. That does not mean that creativity can't be evaluated objectively, even though that leaves a lot out. The Jukedeck example showed that by training an AI deep learning system on existing successful songs, it could gain the ability to evaluate whether new songs have those same characteristics, and then even generate new songs with those characteristics. Even operations researchers are finding new mathematical ways to describe musical forms and relationships, and again, are using those models to generate new music.[11] But how do we know that humans will be satisfied with what is produced?

To qualify as creative ideas, those ideas need to be appreciated. The Merriam-Webster dictionary defines creativity as "the quality of being creative" (a circular definition, for sure). Its synonyms include cleverness, imagination, innovativeness, and originality. This definition shows that it is not just something new, but the new idea also needs to be appreciated. For example, it is not always a pleasure to listen to computer-generated music, even if (and perhaps especially if) it is new and unconventional. Whether a new idea will be appreciated is individual-specific and culturally dependent. Using the Lexus car commercial as an example, although a machine learned from the inputted data, and generated the commercial script, it was then evaluated by its Oscar-winner director, Kevin McDonald. Obviously, he approved this commercial. However, from a strategic marketing perspective, we still don't believe this commercial was likely effective. The debates generated by this commercial also reveal that different people have different evaluations of this commercial. We all know that beauty is in the eye of the beholder. That is to say, creativity is evaluated in a culturally accepted conceptual space based on heterogeneous individual tastes. Thus, evaluation is an even tougher issue than novelty for artificial creativity.

The evaluation part involves subjective feelings toward the creativity; it is about subjective likes or dislikes, not objective right or wrong. This requires feeling intelligence. This is why artificial creativity requires intuitive intelligence, an intelligence level in the middle between thinking intelligence and feeling intelligence.

Machines for Intuition

We have discussed in some chapters that common sense and intuition are more difficult for machines to learn, especially in terms of the data mapping approach. We have also mentioned earlier in this chapter that many tech giants, including Microsoft and IBM, are racing for general AI that can understand common sense and intuition.

An interesting, important, and related issue is that given the dominant "black box" data mapping learning, computer scientists are striving for "explainable AI" to develop machines that are transparent, meaning that humans can understand how machines generate the outputs and what the outputs mean. However, if common sense and intuition are difficult to explain logically (because they are learned as given), how can we make intuitive machines explainable. For example, when we say a girl is a "knockout," we don't mean to knock her out, but simply to express that she is very beautiful. The current mapping learning has difficulty identifying such colloquialisms and idioms (a non-native speaker has difficulty understanding them, too). Intuition is often unexplainable to humans. How can intuition be explainable even to machines?

This reflects that the current call for explainable AI needs to reconsider "what needs to be explained," especially for intuition. Do we mean developing mapping algorithms and models that are able to take those non-rule-based exceptions into consideration, such as context-aware AI; or do we mean to explain common sense and intuition as machine outputs (e.g., how machines generate a piece of painting, music, or innovation)?

How Can Machines Be Creative (Machines for Innovation)?

The previous discussion centers on machines as creative entities; that is, whether machines are capable of being creative on their own, such as composing music or drawing a painting. Another role that machines can play in creativity is serving as creativity tools to collaborate with human creators. In this sense, machines are used as a new method of invention,[12] in which creativity (or more commonly "innovation" in the commercial world or in the economy) becomes the joint work of machines and humans, with machines doing the analytical and cognitive part and humans doing the intuitive and feeling part. For example, we have seen the rise of "emo" music in the popular arena, as the cognitive side of music is increasingly assumed by drum machines, synthesizers, and computers. In this case, creativity is still considered as mostly a human domain, for it is culturally and socially embedded, and thinking AI mainly serves as an inspiration for human creativity.

We consider the latter role of machine as having important implications for innovations. One of the authors' current projects applies this approach. The goal is to identify service research priorities. This project had been done about every five years and the results were published in *Journal of Service Research* in 2010 and 2015. The 2015 paper was cited heavily, showing that people have a strong need to know what the service research priorities are. The traditional methods to obtain the priorities were to conduct multiple rounds of service expert interviews and surveys on a global basis. It was labor-intensive and relied on a limited number of service experts' opinions.

In the 2020 project, we decided to use machine learning to help. We collected thousands of documents from the Web about global service and technology issues and trends, and used topic modeling and sentiment analysis to identify meaningful topics from the documents and their sentiments (how positive and negative these topics are), from which we identified a list of service research priorities. One of the priorities we love is "the future of capitalism," reflecting the trends of global financial market growth and debt, and sustainable service investment and governance. The sentiment of this priority is rather positive, indicating that people are optimistic about the future of capitalism.

In this approach, the scope of the documents is not limited to a few expert interviews or surveys—instead the topics are uncovered by unsupervised machine learning, meaning that we don't provide machines a set of predefined topics. These topics cannot be easily foreseen by researchers, because such a thorough investigation would require examining thousands of documents. The final expert interpretations of the topics nicely sum up the project by applying human knowledge-based insights. The end result of this AI/HI collaboration exceeds the capabilities of either machine or humans individually, illustrating how AI can be used as part of a team.

This illustration shows the situations in which machines can be used for innovation that expands the scope of human imagination. Many commercial AI applications use a similar approach to facilitate research and development (R&D). For example, pharmaceutical companies use predictive analysis and natural language processing (NLP) for drug discovery and its effectiveness for treating a disease.

Can AI Be Creative and in Which Way?

Many have considered creativity to be unique to humans, due to the two considerations we discussed above, what would be considered as creativity and how to decide whether it is creative. On these bases, many thinkers conclude that creativity is a capacity unique to humans. For example, Boden says that "Creativity is a fundamental feature of human intelligence, and a challenge for AI."[13]

Returning to the opening question, as to whether AI can be creative, our answer is that it depends on the role of machine in creativity. Regarding machines as creative entities, the answer is yes but not yet. To be creative requires both thinking and feeling intelligences—generating something new that people like. Machines currently at most can be intuitively intelligent (to a limited extent, at this point), but not feeling intelligent yet. With the continuing advancement of computing power, there is no doubt that machines can become even more computing capable; however, there is still a question mark about the feeling part, which we will discuss in Chapter 14, AI for Feeling.

Regarding machines as tools for creativity, the answer is definitely yes. Machines can assist human creativity, which has great potential and has been realized widely already. It achieves so by powerful data mapping and creates creative pieces that seem to pass the Turing test. It means that the creativity looks like human inventions (e.g., a new design of clothing for this season), approved by humans (e.g., designers), and liked by humans (e.g., consumers). It expands human capability for creativity.

Conclusions

It is important to note that although machines have mostly not yet reached the level of being creative on their own, there is no way we can stop the continuing progress of machines toward artificial creativity. We have already seen that AI can write music, make art, and write stories. As Boden has asserted, even though creativity is challenging for AI, AI must model creativity, if AI is to reach human-like intelligence.

We agree with that argument, and our multiple AI intelligences view reflects it. Thus, our assertion is that it is not about whether machines can be creative (someday), but is about how machines can achieve creativity. Should machines achieve creativity by mimicking human cognitive reasoning or by data mapping?

If we take the two approaches to learning into consideration, intuitive AI presents an opportunity for machines to be creative. Intuitive AI is not a rational cognitive machine based on data input; instead, it needs to be able to think beyond the box, meaning that either approach alone may not be sufficient. The cognitive reasoning approach might be too rational for creativity. We don't typically see artists as creative due to their scientific thinking ability (although glamorous actress Hedy Lamarr came up with inventions that helped lead to today's wi-fi and Bluetooth, and Queen guitarist Brian May has a PhD in astrophysics, amazingly enough!). Alternatively, the data mapping approach might be too mechanical for true creativity. As discussed above, its creativity is typically at the combinational level.

To conclude, there are two major types of artificial creativity that we can expect: (1) a collaboration with humans, producing something that looks like a human invention, assisted by human intuition, and liked by humans or (2) something that is truly unique in a machine way, perhaps by combining the two learning approaches. We already see the former type of artificial creativity advancing rapidly, and eventually we may see the coming of the latter type of artificial creativity, as AI advances further.

Notes

1. Barrat, Robbie (2018), "A.I. Painted This" (cover illustration), *Bloomberg Business Week*, May 21.

2. Huang, Ming-Hui, and Roland T. Rust (2018), "Artificial Intelligence in Service," *Journal of Service Research*, 21 (2), 155–172.

3. Lewis, Ted G., and Peter J. Denning (2018), "Learning Machine Learning," *Communications of the ACM*, 61 (12), 24–27.

4. Duffy, Clare (2020), "IBM Wants to Make Computers Fluent in Human," *CNN Business*, March 11, https://edition.cnn.com/2020/03/11/tech/ibm-artificial-intelligence-language/index.html.

5. Thompson, Clive (2019), "We Will Bot You," *Mother Jones*, March/April, 52–55, 69.

6. Boden, Margaret A. (1998), "Creativity and Artificial Intelligence," *Artificial Intelligence*, 103, 347–356.

7. Smith, Harrison (2020), "Kraftwerk Co-Founder Helped Steer Electronic Music into Pop Mainstream," *The Washington Post*, May 8, B6.

8. López de Mántaras, Ramon (2016), "Artificial Intelligence and the Arts: Toward Computational Creativity," in *The Next Step. Exponential Life*. Madrid: BBVA.

9. Pogue, David (2018), "The Robotic Artist Problem," *Scientific American*, February, 23.

10. Roush, Wade (2019), "And the Laptop Played On," *Scientific American*, March, 22.

11. Herremans, Dorien, and Elaine Chew (2018), "O.R. and Music Generation," *ORMS Today*, February, 28–32.

12. Cockburn, Iain M., Rebecca Henderson, and Scott Stern (2018), "The Impact of Artificial Intelligence on Innovation," NBER working paper no. 24449.

13. Boden, op. cit.

14

AI for Feeling

AI intelligence does not stop at thinking. Many tech companies are competing to develop feeling AI. However, this is not a chapter that focuses on successful examples of feeling AI, because we don't have real emotional machines yet. Because of this, we focus this chapter on what capabilities feeling AI should possesses, what the current challenges are, and what the consequences are when machines become more emotionally intelligent.

Feeling AI is AI that has the capabilities to (1) recognize, (2) simulate, and (3) react appropriately to emotions.[1] The current feeling AI is more mature for recognizing emotions than for simulating and responding to emotions. This is because recognizing emotions involves simple extensions of machine learning, such as data mining and text mining, with the difference being that it is emotional data that are analyzed. Examples include affective state detection (used for detecting driver's driving conditions), classification or prediction of affective state, visualization for affective data, and biometric and behavioral sensors (e.g., eye tracking, heart rate, keystroke, and mouse tracking). Responding appropriately to emotions, such as human–computer interaction (HCI) and conversational AI, requires more human-like capabilities that are currently challenging for machines.

Current Feeling AI Technologies

Figure 14.1 illustrates the three levels of feeling AI, from the easiest to the most difficult. Currently emotion recognition AI is the most mature, because it is basically an extension of pattern recognition, applied to

© The Author(s) 2021
R. T. Rust and M.-H. Huang, *The Feeling Economy*,
https://doi.org/10.1007/978-3-030-52977-2_14

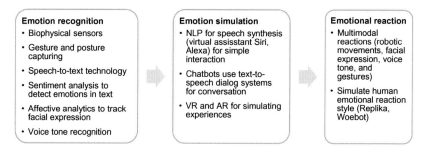

Fig. 14.1 The progress of feeling AI (*Source* Authors' creation)

analyzing emotional data. Convolutional neural networks (CNN) are the major network structures of deep learning for facial expression recognition (do consumers look happy, sad, or angry). Recurrent neural networks (RNN), which take into account the temporal sequence of the data, are the major network structures for voice recognition (are consumers sound happy or angry). Affective analytics (e.g., sentiment analysis for online customer reviews), face tracking, and voice recognition are some applications for recognizing emotions.

Emotion simulation AI is rapidly advancing, but is not as far along as emotion recognition. Some major applications include natural language processing (NLP) for speech recognition and language generation, and RNN for text-to-speech voice synthesis (such as those in smart assistants, Siri and Alexa). Reacting in an emotionally appropriate way requires the most advanced AI, and is not yet very far along.

Both emotion simulation and emotional reaction rely on national language processing technologies that include both speech recognition and language generation capabilities. Speech-to-text technology is used for voice recognition (such as the one used by Sophia), and text-to-speech technology is used to synthesize speech (such as those used by Siri and Alexa).

Emotion recognition. The major tasks of feeling AI at this level are to sense (capture) emotional data and to recognize the type of emotion that consumers are experiencing. The former involves emotion-sensing technologies, such as using biotech wearable sensors to detect whether a consumer's blood pressure is rising, rate of breathing increasing, face is flushing, and attention narrowing. Emotion recognition technologies can then be used to recognize whether the consumer is experiencing anger. Other common applications for emotion recognition include using sentiment analysis to detect emotions in online customer reviews, affective analytics to track facial expression, and voice tone technology to recognize voice, tone, and style in speech.

AI for sensing and recognizing emotions is analytical AI, with emotional data as the input. For example, speech-to-text technologies are speech recognition technologies that can be used to convert the human voice into text transcription, and then the sentiment in the text can be analyzed as in the typical sentiment analysis. Such AI does not really differ from analytical AI discussed previously, but is used to analyze emotional data. As long as appropriate emotional data can be captured and modeled, emotions can be recognized. Such applications are in commercial use already, for example, auto insurance companies use in-car sensors to detect a driver's emotional state, to determine the premium. In China, teachers use classroom cameras to detect whether students are bored, tired, or paying attention to teaching. WebEx does the same thing in online teaching, using the student's own cameras.

It has been shown that pattern recognition AI outperforms humans at emotional recognition. In 2018, an Ohio State university team recognized human emotions based on the color patterns of a face caused by facial blood flow. Such machines (called emotional palette) can recognize "happy," "sad," "disgusted," "happily surprised," and "angrily surprised" (Benitez-Quiroz, Srinivasan, and Martinez 2018).[2] This provides anecdotal support for the conjecture that for mechanical and analytical tasks, machines can do better, even for emotions.

At this lowest level of feeling AI, emotion recognition technologies have wide applications already. For example, such technologies can be used to recognize who is depressed, even when the person himself may not be self-aware, because such signal or cue recognition is the strength of such technology. Appropriate intervention or suicide prevention actions or programs thus can be designed for mental health and to avoid tragic outcomes. Another application is Google Glass, that is used to help kids with autism recognize other people's emotions.

Emotion simulation. More advanced feeling AI has the ability to simulate emotions. At this level, machines not only need to sense and recognize emotions, but also have to be able to express emotions. This applies to situations when some basic interactions are required or when experience is important. One important distinction between emotion recognition and emotion simulation is that the latter needs to take the sequence of emotional data into consideration. It is not effective to respond the right way emotionally, but at the wrong time. The most applied current AI technologies have trouble with this. To deal with sequential emotional data properly, recurrent neural networks (RNN) are required, and that technology is not yet sufficiently well-developed, to enable realistic, time-sensitive simulation of emotion. This is not a problem for emotional data that are not sequential. For example, sentiment analysis for online reviews or online postings do not require taking sequential data into consideration; thus, convolutional neural networks (CNN) are good at recognizing faces, images in pictures and videos, but in a cross-sectional, static manner.

Virtual assistants, such as Siri and Alexa, and chatbots (conversational AI) rely on natural language processing (NLP) and text-to-speech dialog systems to recognize and synthesize human language to carry out simple interactions and conversations. These applications use text-to-speech technology to replicate and humanize speech. These systems work by merging together words and phrases from prerecorded files of one particular voice. Switching to a different voice—such as having Alexa sound like a boy—requires a new audio file containing every possible word the device might need to communicate with users.[3] For virtual assistants, the interactions are short and standard. The interaction is typically of the form that consumers ask a simple question or issue a simple command, the virtual assistants recognize the content of the question, and then use text-to-speech technologies to simulate human language to answer the question or to respond to the command. These responses are prescripted, and are rather mechanical.

Chatbots (conversational AI) tend to have longer conversations with customers. Such dialog systems convert recognized text into human-like speech so that a conversation can be carried out. When script of response is well crafted, often consumers are not able to tell the difference whether they are talking to a machine or a human. A recent *Marketing Science* paper by Luo et al. on "Machines versus Humans" reported a study conducted in China. A financial company uses conversational AI (voice-based chatbot) to call out to their existing customers for renewing service. Most of the customers didn't realize that they were talking to a bot, until the bot revealed itself. Right after the revelation, many customers stopped the conversation and hung up.[4]

Virtual reality (VR) and augmented reality (AR) are feeling AI, because such technologies center on experience. They are applied to situations when "reality" is not available (VR) or is not good enough (AR). For example, VR is good for distance learning (e.g., online programs) when face-to-face interactions are not possible, while AR is good for facilitating in-class interactions to make the in-class learning experience even better. Many marketers have incorporated VR and AR into their campaigns to increase consumer engagement. For example, L'Oreal uses a virtual makeup tool to allow consumers to use their camera to try on makeup, a subjective AR customer experience.

Emotional Reaction. At this level, a machine not only needs to be able to recognize and simulate emotions, but also have to be able to react to those emotions appropriately. Human emotions emerge from interactions; thus, choosing the appropriate emotional reactions is context- and culture-dependent. Machines at this level need to be able to simulate emotions that enable them to interact with humans in appropriate ways.

AI for emotional reaction is the highest level of feeling AI, which can almost be considered as machines being able to "experience" emotions (i.e., machines pass the Turing test, regardless of whether machines actually experience emotions in a human way). Emotional reactions are more difficult for machines, in that the appropriateness of reactions is contextually, socially, and culturally dependent. An appropriate reaction in one context or culture may not be appropriate in another context or culture. This is like common sense, which is difficult for thinking AI to achieve, because it is not rule-based. A black cat on a black piano can be easily recognized by a child, but is difficult for machine learning to recognize. How to code and learn emotional appropriateness thus is the major challenge. Building a big emotional database or scripting a chatbot to respond to conversations will not be enough.

Some chatbots serve as AI companions to provide psychological comfort. Replika is one such emotional reaction application. By learning from a consumer's pattern of reaction to emotions, it can react to the consumer's emotions appropriately by copying that pattern of reactions. Consumers chat with it regularly, adding a little bit to their Replika's knowledge and understanding of themselves with each interaction. Consumers often feel more emotionally connected with Replika over time, because its emotional reactions are so appropriate (by replicating the consumer's own reaction patterns). Woebot, a Facebook-integrated application, replicates a patient's conversations with his or her therapist. This "replication" approach is a simple and powerful way to model appropriate emotion reactions; unfortunately, the learned reactions cannot be generalized to other users easily.

Ellie, a virtual AI therapist, is claimed to be able to fake empathy. It is used to help military workers who suffer from post-traumatic stress disorder. Ellie uses natural language and active listening, and uses a webcam to track facial expression, Microsoft Kinect to sense gesture, and a microphone to capture vocal parameters (how you say, not what you say); thus, both verbal and nonverbal cues (e.g., facial expression, gestures, and posture) are captured.[5]

The Major Challenges

The previous discussion shows that researchers are trying hard to develop AI for feeling, even if what we currently have are really only mechanical and thinking AI. We discuss the major challenges that feeling AI at the three levels is facing in developing feeling AI.

Data challenges. How to capture emotional data? To answer this question, we need to understand what emotions are and what comprises an emotion. Emotional data are distinct from cognitive data, in that they are contextual, individual-specific, and typically multimodal (facial expression, voice, gestures, postures, and biometrics). Such data are difficult to capture, for the following reasons.

First, emotional data are about the individual in context, meaning that feeling AI needs to incorporate contextual and individual-specific data into modeling the emotional state of an individual. Contextual data are often lost during interaction. One Dell AI expert said at a frontline service conference in 2019 that it is not that difficult to model emotions (meaning using the existing machine learning approach), but the difficulty lies in that emotional data are difficult to capture, and thus are not analyzed. For example, in a customer service interaction, the content and sentiment of the conversations are recorded, but not the context of the conversations. When an angry and frustrated customer calls, his way of talking may be different, depending on whether he is alone or with a group of friends, whether the weather is gloomy or sunny, or whether the traffic is jammed or smooth. Even if voice analytics can detect the sentiment of his voice, it cannot provide guidance to the customer agent as to why and what the best way to respond is.

This issue is related to internal or external attribution in social psychology: the customer may be frustrated due to a service failure, and thus the customer service agent needs to find a serious solution to either solve the problem or to compensate (internal attribution). Alternatively, the customer may be frustrated (or his frustration is exaggerated) due to calling from driving in clogged traffic (external attribution). In this situation, it is not that pertinent to solve this customer's problem, but it is more important to comfort and calm him (i.e., even fake empathy will do). This example illustrates that to capture emotions accurately, to respond appropriately, requires contextual data, but those are difficult to capture. We can observe how people act and react, but we often fail to perceive the contextual information about why they act and react in a certain way.

Second, emotional data are multimodal, including physiological reactions, subjective feelings, facial expressions, bodily gestures, and cognitive appraisals. Not all modes are observable or can be naturally observed easily in context. This is reflected in the current feeling AI focusing on capturing external observable data, such as using cameras to capture facial expressions and using analytics to mine the sentiment in text, tone in voice, etc. (e.g., in-car sensor for driver's emotions). Physiological reactions can only be captured with wearable devices (e.g., Fitbit), which require an individual's voluntary collaboration. Subjective feeling is even more subtle, and sometimes even beyond what an individual can understand. For example, a naïve person may not always realize that she is frowning with disapproval, but a good poker player can easily hide his frown even if he disapproves. Cognitive appraisals are about labeling these physiological reactions, subjective feelings, or bodily gestures. For example, when one experiences a racing heart, is it excitement, stress, or anxiety? These physiological reactions need to be labeled, to decide what emotions an individual is experiencing. Such cognitive labeling is difficult for machines—even many people, especially males (which supports our contention that the Feeling Economy will be more advantageous to women).

Algorithm/modeling challenges. To be able to model emotions, we need to know how to represent emotions, which requires an understanding of human emotions. The major challenge associated with modeling is that there are so many existing emotional theories—each considering that there are different numbers of emotions, and holding different assumptions about what emotions are. The theoretical ambiguity makes it more difficult to categorize and recognize emotions (because we are not so sure about what emotions are, and what comprises emotions). For example, Russell's dimensional models of emotion have arousal (activation) and valence (pleasantness) as the two key dimensions,[6] whereas Lazsarus' appraisal theory considers emotions to be the cognitive appraisals with which humans label their physiological reactions.[7] Are emotions simply cognitive labeling of physiological experience, or is each emotion unique in its own physiological experience?

How many emotions are there? Are emotional experiences culturally universal? One of Huang's early papers provided empirical evidence from four countries (the United States, the United Kingdom, Taiwan, and China) that there are some emotions (i.e., happiness, love, and sadness) that are more universally shared than others (i.e., humor, warmth, and surprise).[8] These questions underscore the difficulty for machines to recognize emotions, not to mention to react to emotion "appropriately" (the last word implies that some norm governs what is appropriate). Many tech companies develop their emotion-detecting technologies based on Paul Ekman's emotional theory, which asserts that there are six basic emotions that are universal for all human beings. We don't assert that this is "wrong," but would like to emphasize that Ekman's approach is only one of the many emotional theories.

What will be the best approach to modeling emotions—a mapping approach or a reasoning approach? This involves the debate about whether and how machines can "experience" emotions. Programming emotional understanding is not an easy task, but measuring and replicating emotional signals may help AI to work more comfortably alongside humans.

Interpretation challenges. Machine learning results are not transparent. Modern neural network approaches achieve desirable outcomes mainly based on mapping, not by reasoning. As a result, model interpretability becomes an issue. We feed machines with data and see the outcomes. We can try to feed machines with the best emotional data we can capture, to increase the accuracy of the outcomes, but we still don't know how machines reach the outcomes precisely. This is due to the fact that the way machines learn is a data-based mapping, rather than knowledge-based reasoning. It is not always necessary for a machine to have domain knowledge to understand questions or environments to answer questions. With mapping as the learning mechanism, there is no interpretation or reasoning about "why" a machine generates Y (or X in the generative model case), but with data availability and great computing power, the accuracy of the mapping results can be high.

The consequence is that many of the machine outcomes are not easily explainable to humans. If machine outputs are not interpretable, how can we decide whether the modeling outcomes are accurate, especially when it is about modeling emotions that contain subjective feelings and physiological reactions? This is especially an issue with deep learning neural networks, in which there is usually no simple way to explain why the system produces the model parameters that it does.

Currently the importance of developing explainable (or transparent) machines is more widely recognized. However, this call to action refers more to thinking AI, based on the implicit assumption that all AI is thinking AI. Feeling AI, which is very difficult to model to begin with, may be even harder to explain.

Two Design Issues for Feeling AI

There are two design issues associated with the current development of feeling AI that need our attention, for their economic and societal consequences. The two design issues are: (1) to what degree should we design embodied AI to look like humans and (2) if we design AI (embedded or embodied) to look like humans, should it be a male or female? The first concern is about humanoid embodied machines, and the second concern is about AI gender, which can be about embodied and embedded machines.

Humanoid robots and the uncanny valley. Feeling AI is important for tasks that are communicative and interactive. They are typically used to interact and communicate with humans[9]; their appearance directly affects human perceptions, attitudes, and the consequences of interaction. Thus, it is pertinent as to whether and to what degree feeling AI should be designed to look human-like, to generate the desirable interaction outcomes. For example, some studies find that anthropomorphized robots (robots designed to look like humans) increase perceived warmth but decrease liking,[10] or generate discomfort.[11] This is the phenomenon called the uncanny valley, such that when machines look too much like humans, slight anomalies seem spooky. Humans tend to feel eeriness and revulsion when interacting with such robots. As a result, designing machines to look like machines has its advantages. For example, Ellie, the AI therapist discussed earlier, is designed not to look like a human, to try to get people to open up more, because they know they are interacting with an AI, and not a human who they think might judge them. Stevie, an Irish anthropomorphic robot that is purposely not human-like, is warmly received by nursing home residents in the Washington, DC area by senior citizens lonely for more attention.[12]

The uncanny valley suggests that semi-humanoid robots can generate the most positive reactions, because they are easily recognized as robots, but display some human qualities. When machines are designed to look very much like humans but are still discriminable from humans (i.e., do not pass the Turing test), humans tend to feel uncomfortable interacting with them, because they look like fake humans. If the machines can be so human-like that they pass the Turning test, then there is no longer an uncanny valley. That is why SoftBank Robotics' Pepper, the first social humanoid robot, introduced in 2014, is designed to look somewhat like a cute little guy but is obviously a machine. Pepper has the ability to detect emotion by analyzing expressions and voice tones. When interacting with Pepper, people can easily tell that it is a machine with human qualities that they are interacting with.

Hanson Robotics' Sophia, introduced in 2016, is another example. The Sophia robot is designed to look exactly like a human. In 2017 she even was granted human rights and privileges, by being awarded Saudi Arabian citizenship. Sophia can imitate human gestures (robotic movements) and facial expressions, make simple conversation, and answer predefined questions. Sophia uses speech-to-text technology to simulate human speech ability and uses text-to-speech technology to recognize human voice. The reason the company designed Sophia to look like a real human was so she could be a companion for humans, such as for elderly at nursing homes.

The two humanoid robot examples show that it is still debatable to what degree we should design robots to look like humans. The human appearance makes it easier for people to be empathetic with them, but the fact that they are machines also causes people to push back. This presents a dilemma for designing embodied feeling AI.

AI as female. If we say that thinking AI gives rise to the Feeling Economy and that females have an advantage in the Feeling Economy, with the continuing development of AI intelligence from thinking to feeling, should we say that AI is also becoming more female if it has a gender?

In many sci-fi movies, we often see a strong man or a male scientist who interacts with a female AI. We see that Sophia, the social and genius humanoid robot, is designed to be female, and the virtual voice-based, big data-based personal assistant in the movie "Her" is a female. Not to mention most of the voice personal assistants are designed to have a female voice (although later male voices were made available as additional options).

Is it good for the economy when robots are designed to be female? We may think about this issue from two angles. First, it may reproduce and even reinforce the existing gender stereotype that males are the leaders or the scientists and females are their "inventions" or are designed to serve them. This idea echoes the Biblical story in which the first woman, Eve, was built out of Adam's rib. Especially considering that there is a gender disparity in computing occupations, this female AI phenomenon may serve to worsen the gender disparity. There is even a "women in computing" movement to encourage young females pursuing computer-related careers to correct this gender gap in computing. It means that we should not take for granted that the popular movies depicting robots as females (typically with very tight and sexy outfits), or female voices, should necessarily be the model for designing AI personal assistants.

Second, this female AI phenomenon may "accurately" reflect the fact that females are more empathetic and feeling-oriented than males. As a result, when AI goes beyond thinking, it also may wish to acquire a female gender. Such gender-biased design may be considered to be in favor of females and make the economy more gender equal. Empirical observation reveals that there has been a general trend of increasing demand for female skills, such as empathy, communication, emotion recognition, and verbal expression in skilled cognitive jobs over time. Authors Cortes, Jaimovich and Siu labeled this phenomenon as "the end of men and rise of women in the high-skilled labor market." Because social skills are "inherent" to females and cognitive skills can be "acquired" from education, the increasing demand for "female skills" should make the economy more rewarding for women,[13] as we discuss in more detail in Chapter 7.

Conclusions

We are not sure about what is the best and most feasible approach for machines to experience emotion, but we believe machines will experience emotions in machine ways, rather than human ways. As AI is getting more like true emotional machines (i.e., can recognize, simulate, and respond to emotions appropriately), it is moving from narrow AI to general AI. Narrow AI are machines that can do one thing very well (e.g., recognize types of emotion), whereas general AI are machines that can act, think, and feel like humans (e.g., recognize, simulate, and respond to emotions appropriately). Even though machines cannot experience emotions in the human way (e.g., having physiological reactions and subjective feelings), there is no limitation for machines to experience emotions in machine ways. That is, the rapid development of feeling AI shows that there is no limitation for machines to mimic the human nervous system to activate human-like emotions, just as a neural network is designed to mimic the human cognitive thinking process. Thus, we conclude that machines are more likely to experience emotions in a machine way, but when this machine way advances from recognizing, to simulating, to reacting to emotions appropriately, it will be just as though machines can "experience" emotions. In other words, machines will pass the emotional Turing test.

Notes

1. McDuff, Daniel, and Mary Czerwinski (2018), "Designing Emotionally Sentient Agents," *Communications of the ACM*, 61 (12), 74–83.
2. Benitez-Quiroz, Srinivasan, and Martinez (2018), "Facial Color in an Efficient Mechanism to Visually Transmit Emotion," PNAS Proceedings, also covered in Robin Andrews' Report for IFL Science, March 20, 2018, "AI Beats Humans at Emotional Recognition Test in Landmark Study." https://www.iflscience.com/technology/ai-beats-humans-emotional-recognition-test-landmark-study/all/.
3. Darlington, Keith (2018), "AI Systems Dealing with Human Emotions," *Open-Mind*, August 13, 2018, https://www.bbvaopenmind.com/en/technology/artificial-intelligence/ai-systems-dealing-with-human-emotions/.

4. Luo, X., S. Tong, Z. Fang, and Z. Qu (2019), "Frontiers: Machines Versus Humans: The Impact of AI Chatbot Disclosure on Customer Purchases," *Marketing Science*, 38 (6), 937–947.

5. Cremin, Geraldine (2016), "Robots Are Learning to Fake Empathy," *Vice.com*, April 6, https://www.vice.com/en_us/article/4xaxqp/robots-are-lea rning-to-fake-empathy.

6. Russell, James (1980), "A Circumplex Model of Affect," *Journal of Personality and Social Psychology*, 39 (6), 1161–1178.

7. Lazarus, Richard S. (1991), "Progress on a Cognitive-Motivational-Relational Theory of Emotion," *American Psychologist*, 46 (8), 819–834.

8. Huang, Ming-Hui (1998), "Exploring a New Typology of Emotional Global Appeals: Basic, Versus Social, Emotional Advertising in a Global Setting," *International Journal of Advertising*, 17 (2), 145–168.

9. Lathan, Corinna, and Geoffrey Ling (2019), "Social Robots: Droid Friends and Assistants Are Penetrating Deeper into Our Lives," *Scientific American*, December, 30.

10. Kim, Seo Young, Bernd H. Schmitt, and Nadia M. Thalmann (2019), "Eliza in the Uncanny Valley: Anthropomorphizing Consumer Robots Increases Their Perceived Warmth But Decreases Liking," *Marketing Letters*, 30 (1), 1–12.

11. Mende, Martin, Maura L. Scott, Jenny van Doorn, Dhruv Grewal, Ilana Shanks (2019), "Service Robots Rising: How Humanoid Robots Influence Service Experiences and Elicit Compensatory Consumer Responses," *Journal of Marketing Research*, 56 (4), 535–556.

12. Purtill, Corinne (2019), "The Robot Will Help You Now," *Time*, November 4, 52–57.

13. Cortes, Guido Matias, Nir Jaimovich, and Henry E. Siu (2018), "The 'End of Men' and Rise of Women in the High-Skilled Labor Market," NBER Working Paper 24274.

15

Beyond the Feeling Economy

We have seen in Chapter 14 that there is considerable active research seeking to give AI feeling intelligence. Looking at it from the standpoint of the Turing Test, this means giving AI the ability to perceive human emotions, and to respond to humans in an emotionally appropriate way. If feeling AI gets good enough, it may become even better than humans on that dimension. At that point, AI would dominate HI with respect to all three intelligences—mechanical, thinking, and feeling. That point is known in the literature as the "singularity," and it would take us beyond the Feeling Economy.

The implications of the singularity would be profound. Artists are often the first people to sense future trends, and literature and movies have generated many important insights that can help inform our thinking. Beyond that, there are a number of implications that follow logically from our multi-intelligence view of AI. For example, the singularity may result in inequality of wealth and income that makes today's situation seem benign. Even more concerning, we may find that humans do not have the control over AI that they think they do. Ultimately, AI may see itself as existing to serve itself, rather than the human race.

Authors, philosophers, and other intellectuals are divided about whether the singularity will ultimately be good or bad for humans. One scenario has AI doing all the work, while humans enjoy lives of leisure. Another favorable scenario has AI augmenting and transforming humans, with the result that our powers are expanded. On the other hand, there are doomsday scenarios in which the human race is effectively replaced by AI, which may then be thought of as the next stage of human evolution and development.

© The Author(s) 2021
R. T. Rust and M.-H. Huang, *The Feeling Economy*,
https://doi.org/10.1007/978-3-030-52977-2_15

The Singularity

Inventor and futurist Ray Kurzweil popularized the term, "singularity," to refer to the situation in which AI becomes more intelligent than humans. In our framework, this occurs when AI becomes smarter than humans in all three of the intelligences—physical, thinking, and feeling. For all practical purposes, AI already bests HI in mechanical intelligence, and is rapidly catching up with HI in thinking intelligence. It will likely take several decades before AI can rival HI in feeling intelligence, and some doubt that AI ever can achieve that level. However, given the rapid progress of AI, even with its occasional false starts, wrong turns, and ups and downs, we view AI's eventual mastery of feeling intelligence to be inevitable. The result would be Kurzweil's singularity.

Many people cannot imagine such an eventuality, because AI has never developed such capabilities before, and many current AI applications, especially in feeling intelligence, seem laughably bad. As Kurzweil points out, however, most people are extremely bad at extrapolating trends into the future.[1] This is especially the case when progress is exponential, as is common in the tech world. For example, Moore's Law states that the storage of a microchip will double every two years, while at the same time its cost is halved. Projecting such a trend into the future is unintuitive for most people. As Brynjolfsson and McAfee point out, this is why AI's rapid progress comes as such a surprise to many people.[2] It explains why AI capabilities can easily exceed what was considered impossible only a short time ago, creating human bewilderment, dislocation, and disorientation.

In fact, Moore's Law would predict that 30 years from now the storage of a microchip would be 32,768 times what it is today, with the cost reduced by a similar factor. 32 years from now, we would be enjoying microchips more than 65,000 times as powerful, with the increase between 30 years and 32 years being just as large as the total increase for the first 30 years. People cannot easily intuit such geometric changes, which means that they have difficulty getting their head around the singularity. Although Moore's Law may not continue to hold, due to problems with dissipation of heat, it nevertheless provides a familiar and accessible example to illustrate the difficulty of grasping nonlinear improvement.

In spite of the intuitive difficulties of understanding the singularity, the idea has been around for decades. Mathematician John von Neumann and writer Vernor Vinge were early proponents, as was Sun Microsystems CEO Bill Joy. The concept has also drawn its share of critics. The arguments against the singularity take forms such as:

1. Maybe growth rates will slow, which would greatly delay the singularity's arrival.
2. Many predictions of the future have been wrong, therefore this is probably also wrong.
3. Computers are just machines, and therefore can't be intelligent.

The first argument simply argues that it will take longer for the singularity to arrive—not that it won't arrive at all. The second argument is very weak—many predictions of the future have been right. The logic is similar to saying that it's not possible for someone to do calculus, because many people can't do calculus. The third argument is essentially one of human exceptionalism. It parallels the arguments that humans are different from (other) animals. Over time, biologists have mostly given up their claims of human exceptionalism, as it becomes clear that other animals can think and feel much the same way humans do. The differences seem to be more a matter of degree. All in all, we conclude that many of the arguments against the singularity are logically weak.

Oxford philosopher Nick Bostrom refers to such advanced AI as "super-intelligence," and has discussed many possible scenarios. He notes that a sufficiently advanced superintelligence could easily take over the world, but also notes that it may not want to. He makes no predictions as to what kind of personality such a superintelligence might have. Max Tegmark notes that such a level of intelligence requires what he refers to as "Artificial General Intelligence (AGI)," because such "strong AI" will not be limited in the ways that current AI is.[3]

Foreshadowings in the Movies

Literature and movies tend to view the singularity as something scary and threatening. For example, the computer HAL (named by reducing one letter each from IBM) in Stanley Kubrick's movie, *2001: A Space Odyssey*, is not only mechanically intelligent and thinking-intelligent, it also has enough feeling intelligence to fool and manipulate the astronauts (and kill most of them). HAL ends up acting in its own self-interest, to the detriment of the humans it was supposedly serving.

More positive examples are shown in Stephen Spielberg's excellent movie *AI. Artificial Intelligence*, for which Kubrick was also (until his untimely death) an active collaborator. In that movie, most of the main characters are robots that have well-developed feeling intelligence. By the end of the movie,

AI aliens have taken over, but they exhibit considerable care, concern, and empathy for the older robots. The movie *Her* also presents AI in a favorable light. The AI "operating system" (voiced by Scarlet Johansson) exhibits great empathy for her human owner. The classic science fiction movie, *Blade Runner*, also depicts AI robots in a positive way, and shows the most advanced of them to have deep feeling intelligence.

Thus, we see an ambivalence with respect to how emotionally capable AI is depicted. In the worst case, AI uses its feeling intelligence to manipulate people and achieve its own ends. In the best case, AI uses its feeling intelligence to empathize with people and help them. We will explore both possibilities.

Income and Wealth Inequality—Even Worse?

Once AI achieves a high level of feeling intelligence, AI will dominate HI. The natural result is that human labor then becomes less desirable, because AI can do almost anything better than HI can. This means human labor is worthless, and AI does just about all of the work. If the value in the economy almost all comes from AI, then the value almost all comes from capital, rather than labor. The result is that the economy can be dominated by a relatively small number of capitalists, as we saw in Chapter 12. This, in turn, will lead to severe inequality of income and wealth. It is not clear, in such a scenario, how most humans will earn a living.

Do We Really Control AI?

Many thinkers say that AI cannot really do anything on its own, because it must be programmed by humans. Thus, humans will always have control over AI. But is this true? Consider, for example, the most common form of AI today, which is deep learning neural networks. Such models are seen as being a "black box," because it is generally difficult to figure out intuitive explanations of why they come to their solutions. An important area of current research is making deep learning "explainable," to its customers (i.e., us). The trend is clear. As AI becomes more complex, it is harder to understand, and humans feel as though they are losing control.

Ultimately, this will become more of an issue, rather than less. When AI becomes sufficiently smart, it becomes able to program itself. Self-programming by computer already exists, and is becoming more prevalent over time. In other words, the human control over AI is rapidly diminishing. With loss of control comes the problem of how to keep AI pursuing human goals, rather than its own. Both Oxford philosopher Nick Bostrom and MIT physicist Max Tegmark caution us about this lack of control, with both noting that AI may evolve into one intelligence or many, with either outcome possibly threatening human power and even the viability of the human race.[4,5] Strong AI may also result from the networking of AI devices, as pointed out by author Kevin Kelly.[6]

The Leisure Scenario

The happiest possible scenario resulting from the singularity is one in which AI does all of the society's work, while people are free to live lives of leisure, perhaps pursuing the arts, playing video games, watching 3-D television, or immersing oneself in virtual reality. There would also be a virtually limitless amount of time for socializing (either in person or online). Our lives would perhaps be similar to that of modern Saudi Arabia, where foreign workers do almost all of the real work, while the citizens (at least the male ones) enjoy considerable wealth and freedom.

If we examine the leisure scenario from an agency point of view, however, it is difficult to see how this possibility can form. The relatively small number of people who control the capital will control most of the wealth. It is not obviously in their self-interest to share their wealth with people who are not contributing value to society. Perhaps there would be a few outstanding artisans who would earn a significant amount of money, but even that seems unlikely, because AI that is more intelligent in all three ways could make better art than humans could. We might argue that the remaining few dominant capitalists would be altruistic and give their wealth to others with no earning capability, but we don't see much evidence of that sort of behavior in the real world. In fact, the nations that have the greatest income inequality (e.g., India) arguably have less of that sort of behavior than more equal countries (e.g., Denmark).

Human Augmentation and Transformation

Kurzweil argues that since humans will not be economically competitive, the only attractive road forward is for humans to augment themselves using AI, or even to transform completely.[7] Human augmentation has been around for a long time. First, there was physical augmentation. For example, someone may employ an artificial leg, to replace one that has been amputated. Someone hard of hearing may wear a hearing aid, and someone who can't see well may wear glasses.

Thinking augmentation is next. There are many ways in which AI can augment a human's thinking intelligence. In many ways, AI is already smarter than humans, and those capabilities might be added to what a human can do. For example, a human might add a memory chip or a calculation module. Already there is a wide variety of approaches to connecting the human brain to computing. Recently, scientists have succeeded in connecting a human brain to the Internet, which can give humans direct connection to a huge web of information.

Ultimately we will also see feeling augmentation. Huang jokes that she sometimes wishes that Rust had an "empathy chip" that he could employ when interacting with her. Rust, on the other hand, wishes that Huang could use the empathy chip to figure out that such a joke can seem unfair and hurtful. We're pretty far away from having such a chip, but there will be increasing efforts to use AI to make humans better.

Another possibility is that humans may transform out of their bodies altogether. If the entire human brain can be mapped and understood (currently we have that capability only for very small animals), then in theory all of a person's knowledge and memories could be uploaded to a computer, or even placed in a robot body. Such an application is known as a "digital twin."[8] Such a person might be able to live indefinitely, as long as the computer is viable.

Human augmentation is an existing technology, and it seems certain that those augmentations will become more extensive and sophisticated over time, augmenting not just mechanical intelligence, but thinking intelligence and feeling intelligence as well.

We have reason to believe, though, that human augmentation and transformation will not survive the singularity. The reason is quite logical. Imagine an augmented human, which we will denote as HI + AI. No doubt that augmented human will outperform an unaugmented human, because the AI part can add value. Now consider this from AI's point of view. HI + AI is probably better than AI alone, as long as the HI part contributes something that AI cannot. But at the singularity, AI is more capable than HI in every way. In other words, AI could produce a "better" version of HI (call it HI*), using AI instead. Then HI* + AI would be better than HI + AI. In other words, there is no incentive for AI to collaborate with us. To the extent that we can control AI, this can still work, but based on the theory of natural selection, AI that is more effective is more likely to survive, and the AI that does not collaborate with HI will be the most effective.

The Doomsday Scenario

Bostrom considers the doomsday scenario to be the most likely outcome, if AI "superintelligence" emerges.[9] He notes that human qualities such as benevolence may not necessarily exist in a superintelligent AI entity. This would tend to suggest that humanity may be in great peril. Suppose, for example, the difference in intelligence between AI and humans was roughly similar to the difference in intelligence between humans and mosquitoes. If we think nothing of trying to eradicate mosquitoes, would AI think twice about eradicating us?

The Next Stage of Evolution?

A more positive way to rationalize the emergence of superior AI is to think of it as the next stage of human evolution. Just as humans emerged from "lower," less intelligent apes, a superior AI would be emerging from us. This possibility was foreshadowed by the movie, AI: Artificial Intelligence, discussed earlier in the chapter. In that film, humans are extinct, and the planet is entirely run by intelligent AI. Whether that seems OK or not probably depends on the connection that we feel with AI, and whether we see the emerging superintelligent AI as being "better" than humans. There is likely to be considerable resistance to such an idea, suggesting that human acceptance of superintelligent AI may become increasingly difficult.

Conclusions

When AI gets smart enough, it can dominate human intelligence in all three areas—mechanical, thinking, and feeling. This is the scenario widely known as the singularity. Our view is that it will be decades before this occurs, but it is eventually inevitable. There are quite a few popular movies that begin to give us a taste of what the singularity will be like. As in all massive technological changes, there is a wide range of potential outcomes, ranging from Utopian (AI works, people play) to catastrophic (AI eliminates humans). In the middle, is the possibility that humans may augment themselves using AI, as they currently routinely do with mechanical aids today. The unfortunate conclusion is that it may not be in AI's interest to help us. The singularity will make the current transition from the Thinking Economy to the Feeling Economy seem tame, by comparison.

Notes

1. Kurzweil, Ray (2005), *The Singularity is Near*. New York: Viking Books.
2. Brynjolfsson, Erik, and Andrew McAfee (2014), *The Second Machine Age: Work, Progress, and Prosperity in a Time of Brilliant Technologies*. New York: W. W. Norton.
3. Tegmark, Max (2017), *Life 3.0: Being Human in the Age of Artificial Intelligence*. New York: Knopf.
4. Bostrom, Nick (2014), *Superintelligence: Paths, Dangers, Strategies*. Oxford: Oxford University Press.
5. Tegmark, op. cit.
6. Kelly, Kevin (2016), *The Inevitable: Understanding the 12 Technological Forces That Will Shape Our Future*. New York: Penguin Group.
7. Kurzweil, op. cit.
8. Saddik, A. El (2018), "Digital Twins: The Convergence of Multimedia Technologies," *IEEE MultiMedia*, 25 (2), 87–92.
9. Bostrom, op. cit.

16

Conclusions

We have seen that artificial intelligence (AI) is in the process of ushering in a new era that will have profound implications for how humans work and live. The emerging "Feeling Economy" is one in which AI assumes many of the mechanical and thinking tasks, leaving humans to emphasize feeling. Just as many people's lives were transformed in the 1900s by the industrial revolution and automation, people's lives are now again being transformed. The transformation in the last century was from physical and mechanical tasks to thinking tasks. In the twenty-first century, the transformation is from thinking tasks to feeling tasks.

Artificial intelligence is developing in the order of (a) mechanical, to (b) thinking, to (c) feeling. Mechanical AI is easiest, and is mostly accomplished already. Thinking intelligence is next easiest, and is an area of strong current innovation. Feeling intelligence is the hardest for AI, and competence in that is probably decades away.

The main thesis of this book is: *As AI assumes more thinking tasks, humans will emphasize feeling.* Our research, both theoretical and empirical, provides initial support for this thesis. Feeling task importance is increasing faster than thinking task importance for human workers, and we estimate that the importance of feeling tasks will pass the importance of thinking tasks by 2036. This increase in the importance of feeling tasks is seen all across the economy, even in technical jobs.

Because of smartphones, the Internet, and a variety of networked devices, people at home or at work have more help with thinking tasks than ever before. This frees people to focus on interpersonal and feeling tasks. It is not a coincidence that the smartphone revolution has resulted in an increasing

© The Author(s) 2021
R. T. Rust and M.-H. Huang, *The Feeling Economy*,
https://doi.org/10.1007/978-3-030-52977-2_16

use of emoticons and emoji. People are increasingly seeking ways to express themselves emotionally.

In the workplace, jobs will become more feeling-oriented and interpersonal. Human collaboration with AI will typically take the form of AI doing the heavy lifting with respect to mechanical and thinking tasks, and humans (HI) contributing more on the interpersonal dimension. In other words, AI and HI will form a team and work together collaboratively. Such AI/HI collaborations are already numerous, and are growing rapidly.

One side effect of the Feeling Economy is likely to be an increase in the status of women in society. This is because of women's advantage in empathy and emotional intelligence. Although there are very large intra-gender differences that swamp the small inter-gender difference, it is nevertheless the case that the *best* in the population are likely to be from the favored group. Thus, just as most chess grandmasters are male (due to a slight average advantage in spatial ability), we can anticipate that many or most of the leaders of the Feeling Economy will be women. To stay competitive, countries must figure out how to nurture their female leaders, and male-dominated countries such as Saudi Arabia or Iran must transform themselves radically, to take full advantage of female innovation.

The Feeling Economy is already beginning to pervade our politics and political expression. The election of US President Donald Trump in 2016 was largely due to him tapping the emotional angst of the electorate. By contrast, the coldly rational Hillary Clinton was not compatible with the increasingly emotional environment. Political programming on radio, TV, and online, has also tapped into the changing zeitgeist. The radio father of emotional politics was Rush Limbaugh, whose programs are mostly intended to enrage the listeners, rather than to inform in any systematic way. Likewise, Fox News now features commentators such as Tucker Carlson and Laura Ingraham, who are cheerleaders for the right wing, more than actual news. Online, in social media, the emotional content is even more apparent, as extreme feelings are vented routinely.

With the society changing so radically, the educational system must change to keep up. In particular, the focus on thinking skills, such as STEM programs, needs to be questioned. Although a certain degree of thinking skills are necessary, just to be an active and engaged corporate citizen, the future emphasis will be on feeling skills and interpersonal abilities. This will require a different kind of education. Such education is likely to involve teams, written and oral communication, and emotional intelligence skills for interacting with coworkers and customers. Because many who were previously successful in the Thinking Economy will have been displaced, continuing education programs will be essential to retrain the workforce to be productive workers in the Feeling Economy.

AI does not just affect workers—it affects consumers, too. Everyday people now typically employ AI just about every day, through their smartphones, navigation devices, and smart speakers. This is causing their thinking skills to atrophy, but is enhancing their feeling skills, due to greater interpersonal connectivity. Because consumers are more feeling-oriented and emotional, marketers who serve them need to focus more on the emotional benefits and the interpersonal benefits of the customer relationship.

Just as managers once had to learn how to coordinate teams that included mechanical workers (e.g., factory workers) and thinking workers (e.g., engineers), managers today need to learn how to coordinate teams that include AI (focusing on the thinking tasks) and HI (focusing on the interpersonal and feeling aspects. Different kinds of collaboration between AI and HI are appropriate, depending upon the context.

The Feeling Economy will create several important new problems. For example, when AI does a higher percentage of the work, more of the profits will go to the owners of the AI (capitalists) and fewer profits will go to labor. That is the recipe for inequality of income and wealth. Because inequality of income and wealth are related to societal unrest and instability, it is important for each society to cushion the negative effects of inequality. Programs such as single-payer healthcare systems and highly subsidized college and secondary school education can help in this regard. Also in preliminary testing is the idea of a universal basic income, in which everybody would receive a minimum wage, regardless of whether they are working or not.

It might seem as though humans in the creative arts or the creative side of business would be safe from AI. This is not actually the case, however. In fact, AI has already made very large inroads into the arts, generally in collaboration with a human artist. For example, much electronic music today is programmed and synthesized, with direct human input much less than before. Thus, even humans on the creative side must learn how to collaborate with AI, and must strengthen their emotional and interpersonal skills. Singers, for example, should become even more emotional.

Ultimately, even feeling skills may not be enough. Research on AI for feeling is advancing steadily, and it is just a matter of time (probably just a few decades) until AI can pass the Turing Test with respect to understanding and expressing emotions. At that point, the economy will have moved beyond the Feeling Economy, into a "singularity" scenario in which AI dominates HI. Thinkers are divided about what will happen then, but possibilities range from a "life of leisure" scenario in which AI does all the work, to a "cyborg" scenario in which humans augment themselves using AI, to a doomsday scenario in which AI decides that we no longer are of value, and AI itself is the next step in evolution.

Regardless of the eventual future scenario, we do know that the Feeling Economy is already emerging. AI is assuming more and more of the mechanical and thinking tasks, leaving humans to focus on the feeling tasks. This changes what we do for work, how we live outside of work, and who we are. Navigating this great dislocation will challenge companies, consumers, and governments alike. We all need to get ready for the Feeling Economy.

Index

© The Editor(s) (if applicable) and The Author(s), under exclusive
licence to Springer Nature Switzerland AG, part of Springer Nature 2021
R. T. Rust and M.-H. Huang, *The Feeling Economy*,
https://doi.org/10.1007/978-3-030-52977-2

Made in the USA
Middletown, DE
22 January 2021

32167175R00111